ection 1992:

uide to
S. Foreign
olicy Issues

npartisan briefs
key issues
cing the nation

the Editors of the
reign Policy
ssociation

A s voters prepare to choose a President, the Foreign Policy Association, a private, nonprofit, non-partisan educational organization, has prepared this small volume to inform Americans about some of the most difficult current foreign policy issues facing the country and the next Administration.

FPA's objective throughout its 74-year history has been to help stimulate an informed, thoughtful and articulate public opinion. Americans from all walks of life take part in FPA-sponsored meetings with national and world leaders, and in study and discussion programs based on FPA publications: the annual Great Decisions briefing book, the quarterly Headline Series books and this quadrennial election-year guide. The guide's purpose is to provide the general voter, officeholders, candidates, students and teachers with background information they need to take part in the national foreign policy debate and reach their own informed conclusions.

FPA is convinced that if citizens have access to the facts, no issue is so complex that they cannot understand it. And, by their votes and voices, they will ultimately decide the course of U.S. foreign policy.

We are grateful for the generous grants that made this publication possible.

Election 1992: Guide to U.S. Foreign Policy Issues

Prepared by the Editors of the Foreign Policy Association
New York, New York

★ ★ ★

*This ELECTION GUIDE
has been underwritten by major grants from*

THE
AMERICAN
TOBACCO
COMPANY

American Brands, Inc.

and by contributions from
Michael H. Coles
Marshall B. Coyne
Paul B. Ford, Jr., Esq.
The Gordon and Llura Gund Foundation
Betty Wheeler

Published by the Foreign Policy Association
Chairman: Michael H. Coles
President: R.T. Curran
Editor in Chief: Nancy L. Hoepli
Senior Editors: Ann R. Monjo and K.M. Rohan
Associate Editor: Pamela Gerard
Contributing Editors: Melani Cammett, Joseph R. Gregory, Lawrence G. Potter and Helen J. Simon
Editorial Interns: Aili Marie Piano and Marc Jay Selverstone

Typography and design: K.M. Rohan

Printed in the United States of America
Library of Congress Card Number: 92-72963
ISBN: 0-87124-147-1

Contents

1. Domestic Needs, Global Priorities 5

2. Defense and Security 14

3. Trade and Competitiveness 24

4. Japan and the U.S. 33

5. Soviet Breakup: U.S. Policy Dilemmas 43

6. U.S. Foreign Aid 55

7. The Middle East After the Gulf War 65

8. United Nations and Peacekeeping 76

9. Vietnam and Cambodia 86

10. China and the U.S. 94

11. Global Warming 102

12. International Drug Traffic 111

Index 119

1

Domestic Needs, Global Priorities

✔ *What role should this country play in the world?*
  - *World leader?*
  - *Partner in pursuing democratic ideals and maintaining security?*
  - *Limited partner with goals tailored to immediate security needs?*

✔ *Can the U.S. be a world leader without having its domestic house in order?*

✔ *How can we balance domestic needs and foreign policy priorities?*

BACKGROUND

■ **NEW ERA, OLD DEBATE:** The cold war's end (1947–90) has launched a new era in international affairs and re-opened debate about America's role in the world. The U.S. is now the world's only superpower, its 43-year commitment to contain the spread of communism vindicated by the formal breakup of the Soviet Union in Dec. 1991. Celebration of the collapse of the Soviet threat has been marred by social and economic problems at home. Violent crime, drug abuse and racial tension—dramatized by rioting and looting in Los Angeles in May—trouble many voters in this presidential election year. So do falling educational standards and rising health care costs. They worry about declining prosperity as America's manufacturing base shrinks, its highways and bridges deteriorate, and personal, corporate and government debt widens. Should the U.S. continue to play an activist role in global politics or should it give higher priority to putting its own house in order? Should the U.S. use its wealth and military manpower overseas only when America's interests are directly threatened?

■ **ACTIVISM VS. PRAGMATISM:** Since the American Revolution, citizens have held conflicting concepts of the U.S. and its place in the world. One school of thought holds that America should take an activist role in international affairs. Promoting American power abroad not only benefits U.S. commercial interests, it advances the cause of democracy and freedom in other nations for the common good of mankind. Others favor a more pragmatic approach. If provoked, the U.S. should protect its interests. But the government's first obligation is to preserve the welfare of its people. The U.S. can serve as a model for other nations seeking freedom, but it should neither impose its ideals nor intervene to defend democratic principles overseas.

■ **ISOLATIONISM OR INVOLVEMENT?** Twice in this century—during World Wars I and II—isolationists argued that it was in America's interest to avoid foreign conflicts. During the two decades immediately following World War II, there was a bipartisan consensus in support of U.S. leadership in the global struggle to contain communism. This consensus splintered over U.S. involvement in Vietnam: conservative "hawks" tended to regard the Soviet Union as the greatest threat to world peace; liberal "doves" saw poverty and hunger as greater dangers than communism. The end of the cold war has destroyed the certitude with which Americans view the outside world, and attention has shifted from foreign policy concerns to domestic needs and how to pay for them.

According to a fall 1991 Gallup poll, 71% of all Americans believe that the U.S. should "continue to take an active part in world affairs." This was the highest per-

Moir/Sydney Morning Herald

centage in 26 years. Except for the conservative Republican presidential contender, Patrick J. Buchanan, whose "America First" position is summed up by his rhetorical question: "Why must we pacify the Persian Gulf when women walking dogs in Central Park are slashed to death by bums?," isolationism currently has little appeal. In its strategic "Blueprint" for America, the conservative Heritage Foundation urged that priority be given to fixing up America, but it declared that, "if grudgingly, most conservatives have come to accept that defending America means not only protecting the nation's borders and airspace, but also its global interests." The opposite of isolationism, an interventionist posture that calls for the U.S. to be the ultimate guarantor of the world's security, capable of preventing any collection of friends or unfriendly powers from competing with it, likewise has little appeal.

■ **GO IT ALONE OR COLLECTIVELY?** The current foreign policy debate is primarily between two kinds of realists. (1) One school emphasizes pragmatic self-interest and maintains the U.S. cannot afford the burdens of leadership. It contends that the U.S. must act independently of world institutions in dealing with foreign policy issues, exercise its own judgment and support those governments sympathetic to American values while putting pressure on those deemed hostile or uncooperative. (2) The other school includes those who advocate working with other countries to promote democracy and free trade, solving international problems by consensus and giving stronger support to the United Nations and other such global institutions as the World Bank and the World Court. In his campaign for the Democratic presidential nomination, former Sen. Paul E. Tsongas (Mass.) asserted that "Pax Americana must give way to Heal Thyself." At the same time he called for a "new internationalism" and advocated collective security in which the U.S. is a "major player...but only in reasonable proportion to its allies." Democratic presidential contender Arkansas Gov. Bill Clinton also supports collective action against threats, but argues that the U.S. must be prepared to act alone: "Together where we can, but on our own where we must."

DOMESTIC PRIORITIES

■ **DEFENSE:** The overarching security issue of the past, a superpower confrontation, has been replaced by new concerns, including regional conflicts and the proliferation of nuclear and other nonconventional weapon systems. Military planning is being reoriented accordingly, and defense needs reevaluated. While there is general agreement that defense spending can be trimmed, there are differences over the amount and disposition of the resulting "peace dividend," if any. The Bush Administration has called for a $50 billion defense cut over five years, and would use the savings to lower taxes and reduce the deficit. Governor Clinton has proposed cutting at least $100 billion from the defense budget over the same period and using the savings to repair the nation's infrastructure, improve education and health care, and spend more on other domestic programs, including a job corps. He also promises to reduce the federal government's huge budget deficit. (See Chapter 2.)

THE TAX DOLLAR
(under President George Bush's proposed budget for FY1993)

11¢ to deposit insurance and other federal operations

19¢ to defense

14¢ to net interest payments on government debt

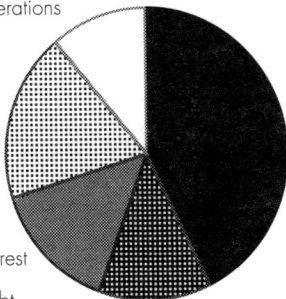

13¢ to states and localities

43¢ for payments to individuals (for Social Security, veterans' benefits, welfare assistance and other programs)

■ **ECONOMY:** Among the serious problems the U.S. faces at home are a $3.8 trillion national debt (up from less than $1 trillion in 1981) and a record budget deficit this fiscal year (FY) of close to $400 billion, compared with $269 billion in FY 1991. In 1990, Congress and the White House cooperated in producing the Omnibus Budget Reconciliation Act, which aimed to cut the budget deficit by $500 billion over five years through tax hikes and cuts in a wide range of government programs. But government spending continues to exceed revenues: the federal government currently spends $4 for every $3 it takes in. The deficit includes $196 billion for net interest on the national debt and $61 billion for the savings and loan bailout.

The continuing deficits led to congressional and White House support in 1992 for a balanced-budget amendment to the Constitution. It failed in June to get the two-thirds vote needed for passage in the House of Representatives.

Pat Buchanan and conservative supporters have called for deep, across-the-board cuts in government spending. They fault the President for breaking his 1988 election pledge not to raise taxes and for failing to reduce the size of government. The White House blames Congress for the deficits. Under the Constitution, the executive branch offers spending proposals, but only Congress has the power to appropriate funds.

■ **U.S. IN GLOBAL ECONOMY:** How serious are the country's economic problems and how do they influence foreign policy? The most pessimistic warn that America's economic decay is so precipitous and increasing foreign competition so damaging to U.S. businesses that the U.S. could soon become a second-rate power. Others argue that the U.S. decline has been overstated. Although the U.S. has given up predominance in several sectors, such as automobile production and consumer electronics, it remains ahead in critical new sectors such as information technology and biotechnology. If one ignores wartime and postwar "blips," they note, the U.S. share of the global economy has remained fairly constant at about 22% to 24% from the 1930s through today.

The U.S. is inextricably linked to the global economy. The lines which used to separate national from global concerns have largely broken down. Pollution, global warming, diminishing natural resources, drug trafficking, terrorism and other problems transcend national boundaries. The revolution in communications, computers and other technologies has speeded the process, and economic interdependence increases daily. Japan, Germany and other trade "rivals" have as great an interest in American economic stability as the U.S. has in theirs. Each country provides a huge market for the others and produces goods and technology that spur the growth of the global economy. The words "Made in USA" have lost much of their meaning. Is an automobile designed in Germany, its parts made in Mexico, and assembled in the U.S., a German, Mexican or American car? Increasingly goods and services today are made to be sold on global, not domestic, markets. (See Chapter 3.) Global stock trading is commonplace. In this global economy, the source of investment matters less than the skills of a nation's work force and the quality of its infrastructure.

ADMINISTRATION POLICY

In the wake of the cold war, President George Bush has advocated that the U.S. take the initiative in establishing a "new world order" based on the following principles:

- The promotion of democracy and free trade.
- A set of rules for international conduct and the means to resist and punish those who violate them.
- Reliance on diplomacy to prevent and resolve disputes, and development programs to enhance support for a more orderly international system.

U.S. cooperation with the the World Bank, the International Monetary Fund and other institutions that provide loans to and encourage investment in developing countries is essential to such a system. Working with the UN to keep the peace and resolve conflicts—and, should that fail, being part of a united military response to aggression—is also crucial. The UN, despite its deficiencies, is still the focal point where the broadest international consensus can be fashioned, tested and translated into action.

The Administration wants the U.S. to have a major rather than a leading role in shaping the new world order. The U.S. "has no intention of striving for a Pax Americana," Bush said in a speech to the UN General Assembly on Sept. 23, 1991. "However, we will remain engaged. We will not retreat and pull back into isolationism. We will offer friendship and leadership. And in short, we seek a Pax Universalis, built upon shared responsibilities and aspirations."

POLICY CHOICES

1. THE U.S. MUST LEAD THE WORLD INTO THE 21ST CENTURY.
YES. (1) Because of its economic power and commitment to democracy, the U.S. is in the ideal position to promote democratic values and free-market capitalism overseas. (2) As the largest economic power and sole nuclear superpower, America has an obligation to take the lead in maintaining peace in the world.

NO. (1) The U.S. cannot encourage democratic values overseas when it is beset by economic and social problems that discredit the country in the eyes of the world. (2) No country alone, not even a superpower, can guarantee peace in the world. Today's global problems require collective solutions.

2. IT IS TIME TO "PUT AMERICA FIRST."

YES. (1) With the cold war won and international tensions easing, it is time to regroup, rebuild and strengthen the U.S. by a massive effort to solve domestic problems. (2) During the Bush-Reagan era, spending on defense and other international priorities rose sharply, while domestic problems grew worse. It is time to reverse the nation's priorities.

NO. (1) America's prosperity is inextricably linked to that of its global partners. Americans cannot afford to turn their backs on the world as they did in the 1930s, when they were so preoccupied with ending the Great Depression that they ignored the rise of fascism, which brought on World War II. (2) America's domestic problems are troubling, but overstated. The U.S. will remain the world's most militarily powerful and wealthiest country well into the next century. It must use its wealth to combat domestic problems, but not at the expense of equally important international interests.

SELECT BIBLIOGRAPHY

Bush, George, "Toward a New World Order." *US Department of State Dispatch,* Sept. 17, 1990, pp. 91–94. Address before a joint session of Congress, Sept. 11, 1990.

Lugar, Richard G., and Wofford, Harris, "Foreign Policy: Decision 92: The Republican Course; The Democratic Challenge." *Foreign Policy,* Spring 1992, pp. 86–99. The authors, both members of the Senate Foreign Relations Committee, offer their views on the goals of their respective political parties.

Nye, Joseph S., Jr., "What New World Order?" *Foreign Affairs,* Spring 1992, pp. 83–96. The author argues for a U.S. foreign policy that promotes American democratic, free-market values.

Tonelson, Alan, "What is the National Interest?" *The Atlantic,* July 1991, pp. 35–52. The author argues that the U.S. should disengage from excessive involvement overseas and concentrate on solving its domestic problems.

"U.S. Agenda for the 90's: Domestic Needs, Global Priorities." *Great Decisions 1992,* pp. 3–12. New York, Foreign Policy Association, 1992. A nonpartisan look at differing views on how America should approach the postcold-war world.

2

Defense and Security

✔ *Do you favor a large reduction in the defense budget? What would you cut?*

✔ *How would you spend the money saved?*

✔ *The Administration plans to reduce the number of active troops by a quarter million by 1995. Is this too much too soon or not enough?*

✔ *How large a nuclear stockpile would you keep?*

BASIC FACTS

- **Defense spending as % of gross domestic product (GDP):**
  - 12% during height of cold war (1950s and 1960s)
  - 6.5% in fiscal year (FY) 1986, peak year of Reagan military buildup
  - 4.6% in FY 1993 (projected)
  - 3.6% in FY 1997 (projected)

- **Defense budget:**
  - FY 1992 budget: $291 billion
  - FY 1993 proposed budget: $281 billion (inflation-adjusted decline of 4.5%)

- **Troops on active duty:**
  - 1987: 2.2 million
  - 1991: 2 million
  - 1992: 1.9 million

- **Strategic nuclear warheads:**
  - U.S.: 11,602
  - Former U.S.S.R.: 10,877

BACKGROUND

For 43 years, U.S. military strategy, defense spending and overall foreign policy revolved around the "containment" of the Soviet Union. Now the Soviet Union has disintegrated. Defense analysts no longer fear a surprise Soviet nuclear attack or worry that a conventional, World War II-style conflict will break out in Europe. These revolutionary changes make it necessary for the U.S. to reorder its foreign, strategic and economic priorities. There is general agreement that military spending should be cut, but not about which programs to trim, how much to cut them, or how to spend the "peace dividend."

■ **WHAT THREATS? WHAT RESPONSE?** During the early 1960s, Robert S. McNamara, defense secretary under Presidents John F. Kennedy and Lyndon B. Johnson, developed the two-and-one-half war scenario. This strategy called for the U.S. to be prepared to fight the Soviet Union in Europe, a full-scale war in the Middle East or Asia, and a smaller one, possibly in Latin America. Today, many analysts doubt that the U.S. would ever face such threats all at the same time. But they disagree on the nature and scope of the potential threats the country does face and how to meet them.

- One option calls for the U.S. to remain strong enough to fight two regional wars at once against, say, Iraq and North Korea, while maintaining enough power to face down an economically revitalized Russia seeking to expand in Europe.

- Another option calls for the U.S. to reduce troop levels drastically and to rely on nuclear weapons to deter war. The U.S. would rely on lean, mobile rapid deployment forces to deal with sudden threats to U.S. interests overseas—for example, a coup in the Philippines, endangering the lives of Americans living there, or political violence in Central America that could close down the Panama Canal.

- A third option calls for the U.S. to place greater reliance on collective security: it would look to the United Nations Security Council to resolve international disputes, support UN peacekeeping forces to combat violence in international hot spots such as the Middle East, and encourage other industrialized democracies to do the same.

■ **MILITARY BUDGET:** President George Bush proposes cutting defense spending by 20% over five years (FY 1992–97). This represents an inflation-adjusted $50 billion less than the $1.42 trillion originally proposed by his Administration in 1991. The savings will come mainly from canceling such weapons as the Seawolf attack submarine ($17.5 billion) and building only five more B-2 "Stealth" bombers at more than $1 billion apiece for a total of 20. The FY 1993 request includes $5.4 billion for the Strategic Defense Initiative, or "Star Wars" program. Congress is expected to trim the request by $1 billion or more. The program's cost this year is $4.2 billion.

Presidential candidate Arkansas Gov. Bill Clinton, a Democrat, would cut the defense budget by more than a third in five years, or $100 billion more than the current Bush plan. He would stop production of the B-2 bomber and cancel Star Wars but not the Seawolf submarine.

Rep. Les Aspin (D-Wis.), chairman of the House Armed Services Committee, would double the Administration's cuts. Democratic presidential aspirant former California Gov. Jerry Brown would go further, reducing the budget to $150 billion by 1997, compared to Aspin's target of $230 billion and the Administration's of $250 billion.

A Brookings Institution study concludes that the U.S. could reduce military spending by more than 33% from current levels over the next decade and still remain the world's strongest military power.

■ **MANPOWER AND FORCES:** The Bush Administration calls for a reduction in military manpower to a "base

"This one is for de-commissioning three nuclear subs, this one is for scrapping fifty strategic bombers, this one is for dismantling one hundred nuclear warheads . . ."

force" of 1.6 million active troops by 1995—down from 2.2 million in 1987. Under this plan, the number of Army divisions would be cut to 12 active and 6 reserve (down from a total of 28 at the end of the 1980s). The Navy would be pared from 14 to 13, possibly 12, aircraft carriers and from 545 to 451 ships. The Air Force would drop from 36 to 26 active and reserve tactical fighter wings. The Marine Corps would maintain 3 active and 1 reserve divisions, but each division would have fewer troops.

Overseas, the Administration would reduce the number of U.S. military personnel stationed abroad from 414,000 at the end of 1991 to 303,500 by 1995: 128,500 in the Pacific, 25,000 in Southwest Asia, and 150,000 in Europe (down from the cold-war peak of 350,000 and the current level of 220,000). The Administration sees a strong U.S. military presence in Europe and Asia as a stabilizing force. It plans to maintain its commitment to the North Atlantic Treaty Organization (NATO), which it considers the main framework for security in Europe, and to continue stationing troops in South Korea, Japan and elsewhere to protect its own interests, as well as those of its allies.

Representative Aspin, among others, calls the Administration's defense plans out of date—a response to the collapse of the Soviet Union's Warsaw Pact military alliance but not to the final breakup of the Soviet Union itself in Dec. 1991. He would reduce the armed forces to 1.4 million and make deeper cuts in the Army's active divisions (to 9 rather than 12) and the Air Force's tactical fighter wings (to 10, not 15) and favors a 340-ship Navy.

Governor Clinton favors strengthening the capacity to move U.S.-based troops quickly and would work to develop a UN rapid deployment force. He advocates continued U.S. support for NATO but with fewer troops in Europe. He would also continue a U.S. military presence in Asia.

Conservative Republican Pat Buchanan would reduce military commitments overseas but favors a strong base force in the U.S.

Other analysts would cut the base force to 1.2 million by FY 2000 and the number of troops in Europe to 100,000 or even 50,000. Former Governor Brown would reduce U.S. troops in Europe to 25,000 or fewer.

■ **BASES, JOBS AND POLITICS:** The President does not have unilateral power to close U.S. military bases; congressional approval is required. Secretary of Defense Dick Cheney has criticized Congress for dragging its feet on base closings and states that defense is not a jobs program.

Many congressmen are loath to eliminate bases or cut weapons procurement in a recessionary period, particularly when it affects jobs in their own districts. (Large metropolitan areas may more readily absorb layoffs than small communities that depend on a single industry, such as Groton, Conn., where the Seawolf submarine is produced.)

Some 2.8 million Americans work in industries

financed by military contracts. Of those, about 500,000 workers are actually making weapons. Analysts estimate that projected budget cuts would eliminate no more than 10% of these jobs. Provided the cuts are not precipitous, reductions in defense spending would not damage the national economy, according to congressional researchers. Because many of these positions involve skilled labor, most of these workers qualify for jobs in other industries. A Feb. 1991 Congressional Budget Office study found that previously planned cuts in defense spending would *increase* employment in the long run, provided the reductions were used to cut the federal budget deficit.

■ **PEACE DIVIDEND:** Under the Omnibus Budget Reconciliation Act of 1990, defense savings cannot be used to finance domestic programs or pay for tax cuts. They can only be used to reduce the federal budget deficit. Intended to trim the budget deficit by $500 billion over five years, the act sets limits on defense, foreign aid and domestic spending and bars transfers between these three budget items.

In 1991, Representative Aspin and Sen. Sam Nunn (D-Ga.) proposed setting aside up to $1 billion of the military budget for humanitarian aid to the Soviet Union. They met bipartisan opposition. Opponents argued the funds should be spent on poor Americans. They also warned that diverting defense funds for nondefense purposes would set a dangerous precedent. Nevertheless, Congress subsequently approved the transfer of $500 million from the FY 1992 defense budget to the Soviet Union—$100 million for transportation of humanitarian aid and $400 million to help the Soviets dismantle nuclear weapons.

A Democratic move in the House to break the 1990 budget agreement and shift more than $6 billion in military savings to social programs was defeated in March 1992 under threat of a White House veto. The vote was 238–187. Unless the cap on domestic spending is removed, critics claim, there is little incentive to halt the funding of unneeded weapons. However, military savings could be used to convert defense industries to civilian use and for retraining. There is some support among congressional Democrats to set aside $1 billion for defense conversion.

■ **NUCLEAR ARMS STRATEGY** is in the midst of the largest rethinking in the history of atomic weapons. In July 1991, Presidents Bush and Gorbachev signed the strategic arms reduction treaty (Start) to reduce each nation's stockpile of roughly 11,000 strategic nuclear warheads by about 30% over the next seven years. After the failure of the Aug. coup by Kremlin hard-liners to depose Mikhail S. Gorbachev, the White House announced a unilateral plan to greatly reduce the U.S. nuclear arsenal by scrapping intercontinental ballistic missiles (ICBMs) with multiple warheads as well as short-range missiles and other so-called tactical weapons designed for battlefield use. Gorbachev responded that the Soviets would also unilaterally reduce their nuclear warheads.

Bush submitted Start to the Senate for ratification in Nov. 1991. A vote on the treaty is expected this year. Start's critics, worried about potential anarchy in the former Soviet Union, urge the U.S. to delay ratification until the political situation there stabilizes. The Commonwealth of Independent States (consisting of 11 former republics of the Soviet Union) has promised to honor the Kremlin's Start commitments. (See Chapter 5.)

■ **NUCLEAR STOCKPILES:** Russia's president, Boris N. Yeltsin, twice proposed reductions in the nuclear arsenals of both countries to around 2,500 warheads. The Administration is prepared to reduce America's nuclear stockpile to between 4,000 and 5,000 warheads.

A National Academy of Sciences report calls for reducing the U.S. arsenal to 3,000 warheads in the immediate future and to 1,000 warheads later on. This will still give the U.S. a powerful retaliatory force, argues the private, nonprofit Center for Defense Information, which maintains that a halt to the U.S. nuclear weapons program (including research, development, testing, production, support for delivery systems and other war-fighting preparations) would slow the spread of dangerous technology, spare the environment further damage and save more than $60 billion a year.

Other analysts argue that the U.S. must preserve its lead in nuclear weapons and technology, which, once lost, would be difficult to regain. America's best defense, they state, remains a good defense. Although it is unlikely that Washington would decide to launch a nuclear strike, some experts maintain that a policy of deliberate ambiguity about "first use" is in the U.S. interest. A hostile nation, they say, will think twice about attacking the U.S. if it knows retaliation is certain.

■ **HOW TO STOP NUCLEAR PROLIFERATION** is the subject of growing debate. Five nations have officially declared that they possess nuclear weapons—the U.S., Britain, China, France and the former Soviet Union. (The Soviet nuclear weapons are based in Russia, Ukraine, Belarus and Kazakhstan. They reportedly are under Russian control, and the other three republics have agreed to return the weapons to Russia.) In addition to the Big Five, India is known to have tested a nuclear device in 1974. Israel and Pakistan are suspected of having undeclared nuclear weapons. Iraq and North Korea, one of the few surviving hard-line Communist dictatorships, are said to be close to developing them. Several other countries have the capability.

All the declared nuclear-armed powers with the exception of France have signed the Nuclear Nonproliferation Treaty (NPT), and France is expected to do so shortly. The nonweapons signatories, who promise not to acquire nuclear arms and have signed a safeguards agreement with the International Atomic Energy Agency (IAEA) obliging them to open their nuclear facilities to IAEA inspectors, include Argentina, Brazil, South Africa and North Korea.

The U.S. is trying to halt the spread of nuclear technology in the former Soviet Union and strengthen nuclear export controls worldwide. Progress toward that end was made in April 1992 when 27 nations signed an agreement setting out rules meant to limit the sale of machinery and material that can be used for making atomic bombs. The U.S. also supports UN inspections of nuclear facilities in Iraq and North Korea. In March, Iraq indicated that it would comply with a UN order to destroy its ballistic missile equipment, as required under the terms of the resolution that ended the Persian Gulf war, and agreed to provide details of its nuclear weapons program. The move came after the U.S. and Britain hinted that they would use military force if the Iraqi government continued to refuse to cooperate with the UN.

POLICY CHOICES

1. MILITARY SPENDING:
A. Cut military spending by 20% over the next five years.
OR
B. Cut military spending by 33% or more in five years or less.

2. TROOPS:
A. Cut troops based overseas but maintain treaty obligations and the ability to intervene militarily when direct U.S. interests are threatened.
OR
B. Bring most of the troops home and rely more heavily on rapid deployment forces.

3. PEACE DIVIDEND:
A. Use savings from military cuts to reduce the budget deficit.
OR
B. Use savings from military cuts for education, job training, health care, infrastructure, environmental cleanup.

4. NUCLEAR ARMS:
A. Keep the U.S. nuclear edge by continuing to test nuclear weapons and build the Star Wars program, while pursuing arms control agreements.

OR

B. Continue to reduce the U.S. nuclear stockpile, scrap the Star Wars program and halt the proliferation of nuclear weapons through the UN and IAEA.

SELECT BIBIOGRAPHY

Adams, Gordon, *The Role of Defense Budgets in Civil-Military Relations.* Washington, D.C., Defense Budget Project (777 N. Capitol St., NW, Suite 710, Washington, DC 20002), April 1992. A basic introduction to the U.S. defense budget process published by an independent, nonprofit research organization established in 1983.

"The Future of U.S. Strategic Forces," *The Washington Quarterly,* Autumn 1991, pp. 133–201. Four analysts look at America's post-cold-war defense strategy.

Hartung, William D., "Curbing the Arms Trade: From Rhetoric to Restraint." *World Policy Journal,* Spring 1992, pp. 219–47. The author criticizes the Bush Administration for failing to seize the initiative in promoting policies that would limit arms exports.

Kennedy, Paul, *The Rise and Fall of the Great Powers: Economic Change and Military Conflict from 1500 to 2000.* New York, Random House, 1987. An eminent historian examines the reasons behind the decline of Imperial Britain and other great empires and compares their problems with those facing the U.S. today.

Nixon, Richard M., "Is America Part of Europe? *National Review,* March 2, 1992, pp. 26–31. The former President, in an excerpt from his new book, *Seize the Moment,* calls for the U.S. to strengthen and expand NATO.

3

Trade and Competitiveness

✔ *Should the U.S. promote free trade or retaliate against those who play by different rules?*

✔ *Should the U.S. protect its industries by raising tariffs?*

✔ *Will regional trading blocs benefit or hurt the U.S.?*

BASIC FACTS

- The U.S. is the world's largest economy, producing 23% of all industrial goods.

- The European Community (EC), with 345 million people, will replace the U.S. as the world's largest consumer market in 1993 when it completes the transition to a single market, with no trade restrictions among its 12 member-states.

- Major U.S. trading partners (in order of importance): Canada, Japan, Mexico, Britain and Germany. Largest regional trading partner: East Asia and Pacific.

- U.S. balance of trade: from 1891 through 1970, U.S. had a surplus. Since 1970, U.S. has had deficits every year except 1973 and 1975. U.S. trade deficits in late 1980s hovered around $170 billion. In 1991, deficit narrowed to $66.2 billion, smallest shortfall in eight years.

- In 1991, the U.S. regained the lead it had lost to Germany in 1990 as the leading exporter of goods.

- One in six American manufacturing jobs is due directly or indirectly to exports.

BACKGROUND

Foreign trade fueled U.S. economic expansion during the early years of this century. But decades of robust growth came to an abrupt halt with the stock market crash of 1929. Today, many historians agree that the Great Depression of the 1930s was induced by protectionist moves in the U.S. and other countries to insulate domestic markets from foreign competition. The dismal economic climate of the 1930s played a large part in setting the stage for World War II. Recognizing this fact, the U.S. and the other industrialized, non-Communist nations worked to promote free trade in the immediate postwar period. In 1947, the General Agreement on Tariffs and Trade, or GATT, was set up as a forum for setting rules and principles governing international trade and eliminating tariffs, quotas and other barriers. Since then, GATT has sponsored eight sets of trade negotiations. The first seven rounds of talks lowered average tariff rates from 40% in 1947 to roughly 5% today. During that period, world trade volume increased by a factor of 20.

■ **URUGUAY ROUND:** The U.S. is currently participating in the eighth round of multilateral negotiations under GATT, whose 108 members produce 90% of the world's trade. The goal of the talks, which began in Punta del Este, Uruguay, in Sept. 1986, is to lower worldwide tariffs by 33% from 1986 levels, limit unilateral import restrictions, and apply free-trade rules to agriculture and financial services. The talks also seek to establish rules governing intellectual property rights, services and investment. Known as the Uruguay Round, these talks were scheduled to end in Dec. 1990 but were prolonged by disagreements between the U.S. and the EC over government subsidies to farmers. The U.S., joined by other food-exporting countries such as Argentina, Australia and Canada, maintains that subsidies give EC farmers an unfair advantage in international markets. Farmers in France, Germany and elsewhere in Europe constitute powerful voting blocs, and European politicians are wary of appearing to cave in to foreign pressure. The U.S. wants the EC to reduce subsidies to agricultural exports by at least a third. The EC has offered to cut them by 18%. Arthur Dunkel, director-general of GATT, has suggested a 24% cut over the next six years.

The talks are not likely to be completed before the Nov. presidential election. If they succeed, they will have far-reaching effects on global and domestic trade. If they fail, the U.S. and other industrialized countries are likely to put greater emphasis on seeking regional and bilateral agreements. And pressure will mount for Congress to implement tougher trade regulations and restrictions on those nations deemed to use unfair practices.

PROTECTIONISM OR FREE TRADE?

Traditionally, the U.S. has espoused a laissez-faire view of commerce: business functions best if left to its own devices with minimal government intervention. Now, however, with concern growing that the U.S. is losing its competitive edge and its position as the world's strongest economy, some Americans think the government should be more active in helping U.S. businesses compete. Others favor protecting U.S. industries against foreign competition by placing unilateral restrictions on imports, and still others, a middle ground between protectionism and free trade.

Conservative Republican Patrick J. Buchanan and liberal Democrat Jerry Brown, former California governor and a presidential hopeful, have called for quotas and other measures to protect ailing U.S. industries and give them a chance to regain strength. Competition from Japan is particularly worrisome to many: House majority leader Richard A. Gephardt (D-Mo.) would give Japan five years to eliminate its trade surplus with the U.S. or face deep cuts in car exports. Arkansas Gov. Bill Clinton, the Democratic presidential candidate with the strongest free-trade position, favors the federal government working in partnership with industry to develop manufacturing jobs, attract foreign investment and push exports.

The U.S. has removed barriers to most imports, but in response to lobbying by industry, labor and special interest groups, Washington maintains some restrictions on trade. For example, U.S. sugar quotas more than double the price of sugar for the consumer. The U.S. also limits imports of peanuts and dairy products. Under the Multifiber Arrangement, a 1973 international accord governing trade in textiles, exporters of apparel and textiles agree to limit shipments to the U.S. The Administration has negotiated "voluntary agreements" with Japan limiting Japanese exports of semiconductors (since 1986), automobiles and auto parts. Americans pay as much as $75 billion a year more for goods due to import fees and restrictions—nearly a sixth of the nation's annual import bill of $490 billion—according to James P. Bovard, a Washington trade analyst cited in *The New York Times*.

REGIONAL TRADE BLOCS

By the end of 1992, when the last trade barriers are removed and goods, services and labor cross borders freely, the EC's 12 member-states will become a single market. In Dec. 1991 in Maastricht, the Netherlands, the EC leaders made another major move toward economic integration when they agreed to take steps to establish a common currency by 1999 at the latest. They also agreed to work toward political integration, including adoption of common foreign, defense and security policies. The Maastricht Treaty requires ratification by all 12 members to come into force. Denmark's rejection in a close referendum in June 1992 technically renders the agreement moot.

The 12-nation EC agreed in principle in Oct. 1991 to join with the members of the European Free Trade Association (Austria, Sweden, Norway, Finland, Iceland, Liechtenstein and Switzerland) in forming a new trade bloc, a European Economic Area (EEA). The accord, which is subject to ratification by national parliaments and the European Parliament, will allow the free flow of most goods, services, labor and capital and will go into effect just as the EC's single market is formed, Dec. 31, 1992. The EEA would be the industrial world's largest trading bloc, with a market of 380 million people. In addition, Austria, Sweden and Finland have applied for EC membership, and Switzerland may follow.

■ **NORTH AMERICAN FREE TRADE AGREEMENT:** The U.S., Canada and Mexico are stepping up talks on a North American Free Trade Agreement (Nafta) covering tariffs, agriculture and investments. Expanding an accord between the U.S. and Canada which went into effect in Jan. 1989, Nafta would be the first comprehensive free-trade pact between two major industrial countries and a major developing country. Many American business organizations support the proposal, which would end many restrictions on investing in Mexico and reduce production costs for U.S. manufacturers who take advantage of Mexico's lower wages. But many labor leaders say it will cost America jobs. Some environmental groups, such as the Sierra Club, fear that Nafta will lead to Mexico's rapid industrialization without environmental safeguards, resulting in more pollution. But others, such as the Environmental Defense Fund, support Nafta, maintaining that it will ultimately raise environmental standards.

There are other sticking points. Mexico is reluctant to allow foreign investment in some oil industry activities. In the automobile industry, there is disagreement over "rules of content" and origin that determine which goods were truly made in the U.S. and Canada. American automakers want a local content of 60% to discourage Japanese rivals from using Mexico as a base for more exports to the U.S. market. Mexico and Canada fear such a measure would drive off the foreign investment they wish to attract.

■ **ENTERPRISE FOR THE AMERICAS INITIATIVE:** The Admin-

Speech bubbles and labels within the cartoon:
"HOLD IT, MANUEL — THERE IS SOME-THING WRONG WITH THIS PICTURE."

GM MEXICANO AUTOFABRICA

"TELL ME, ARE THEY HIRING U.S. BUSINESS EXECUTIVES?" "NOT IF THEY VALUE THEIR FUTURE, THEY AIN'T!"

THEIR DOMESTIC ECONOMY A SHAMBLES, WORKERS STREAM ACROSS THE RIO GRANDE IN SEARCH OF WORK...

istration sees Nafta as a building block for a "new world order" because it will promote America's free-market values overseas and serve as a first step in the creation of its Enterprise for the Americas Initiative. The initiative, introduced by President George Bush in June 1990, seeks ultimately to establish a free-trade zone from Alaska to Argentina, encompassing more than 700 million people. It calls for reducing U.S. tariffs for many Latin American exports, forgiving some of the $12 billion in debt owed by Central and South American governments, and creating a $1.5 billion fund to support market-oriented reform and promote investment.

■ **ASEAN FREE-TRADE AREA:** In response to the EEA and Nafta, the Association of Southeast Asian Nations agreed in Jan. to attempt to integrate its economies. The six-member association, comprising Brunei, Indonesia, Malaysia, the Philippines, Singapore and Thailand, covers a market of nearly 330 million people and has some of the world's fastest growing economies. The accord, which takes effect on Jan. 1, 1993, calls for members to reduce tariffs on a wide range of goods to no more than 20% in five years and 5% by the year 2008.

Many observers welcome the move as one that will promote global trade, but others are concerned that regional trade blocs mean tougher competition for the U.S. and discrimination against products produced outside the region, resulting in a reduced flow of trade.

ADMINISTRATION POLICY

In his 1988 campaign, President Bush declared that he would adhere to the country's traditional free-trade policies. In line with this approach, the Administration has continued to support GATT and is promoting the formation of Nafta. The Bush Administration maintains that a Uruguay Round agreement is important to its free-market goals. Removing trade restrictions would allow U.S. businesses and farmers to sell more abroad, creating more jobs and wealth at home and lowering domestic consumer prices. If the Uruguay Round fails to achieve its goals, the White House has asked Congress to set aside funding for agricultural export subsidies.

Others argue that multilateral free trade is not necessarily in the best interests of the U.S. Under GATT, for example, the Multifiber Arrangement is to be phased out by the year 2003. The American apparel and textile industries claim the elimination of all current MFA quotas would cost hundreds of thousands of American jobs and force a major industry retrenchment.

The Bush Administration hopes to complete negotiations on Nafta before the Nov. election: it "can stand as a practical commitment by the U.S. to help support nations, in Latin America and elsewhere, that are struggling to adopt outward-looking market economies and democratic political systems," says Robert B. Zoellick of the U.S. State Department.

POLICY CHOICES

1. THE U.S. MUST CONTINUE ITS HISTORIC COMMITMENT TO FREE TRADE.

YES. Despite problems, free markets have been shown to be the most effective means for achieving prosperity and preserving democracy. When other nations embrace these values, Americans benefit from lower consumer prices, broader choice of goods, and more foreign investment. Growing global prosperity, particularly in the developing nations, increases chances for world peace.

NO. The U.S. must protect itself from unfair traders. It can do this by imposing tariffs, quotas and other measures on the industries of those countries that do not grant U.S. companies equal access to their markets.

2. THE FEDERAL GOVERNMENT MUST ADOPT A POLICY OF MANAGED TRADE.

YES. The U.S. should emulate Japan, Germany and other countries whose governments take a firmer hand in guiding their industries. It should work to attract foreign investment as well as push exports by American manufacturers.

NO. If Washington played a larger role in shaping industries through such programs as skills training and tax breaks for new businesses, it would result in a widening deficit and more taxes, depleting funds for private investment. Also, choosing which industries to support can be risky.

3. THE U.S. SHOULD CONTINUE TO SUPPORT NAFTA AND THE ENTERPRISE FOR THE AMERICAS INITIATIVE.

YES. Both moves help push free-trade values, lower consumer prices, and provide development opportunities in countries stricken by poverty and political unrest.

NO. Such trade blocs promote a "fortress" mentality and undermine the free-trade principles of GATT. They also increase the chances for wealthier nations to exploit less-developed states.

SELECT BIBLIOGRAPHY

Brown, George E., Jr., Goold, J. William, and Cavanagh, John, "Making Trade Fair: A Social and Environmental Charter for North America." *World Policy Journal,*

Spring 1992, pp. 309–27. The authors offer their prescription for avoiding potential problems in Nafta.

Hakim, Peter, "President Bush's Southern Strategy: The Enterprise for the Americas Initiative." *The Washington Quarterly,* Spring 1992, pp. 93–106. A critical look at the Bush Administration's plans to develop a free-trade zone with Latin America.

Reich, Robert B., "The Real Economy." *The Atlantic,* Feb. 1991, pp. 35–52. America's leaders have not grasped the fundamental changes in the new world economy, the author argues. To maintain its competitive edge, he writes, the U.S. must develop the skills of its citizens and repair its weakening infrastructure.

Zoellick, Robert B., "The North American FTA: The New World Order Takes Shape in the Western Hemisphere." *US Department of State Dispatch,* April 13, 1992, pp. 290–95. Summary of the Bush Administration's views.

4

Japan and the U.S.

✔ *Is the U.S. losing its place as the world's leading economic power to Japan?*

✔ *In the post-cold-war era, will Japan be an ally or a threat?*

✔ *Should the U.S. step up pressure on Japan to assume greater global responsibilities?*

THE COUNTRIES COMPARED:

	JAPAN	U.S.
Population	123.6 million	250.4 million
People per sq. mile	324.5 million	26.3 million
Per capita GNP	$21,830	$17,110
Exports to U.S./Japan	$89.7 billion	$48.6 billion
Balance of trade, U.S./Japan	$41.1 billion	($41.1 billion)

Source: *Handbook of Economic Statistics, 1991*. CIA, Washington, D.C., Sept. 1991.

BASIC FACTS

■ The U.S. and Japan manufacture nearly 40% of the world's goods.

- The U.S. is Japan's most important foreign market; Japan is America's most valuable foreign market after Canada.

- The U.S. trade deficit with Japan is narrowing (down from $60 billion in 1987).

- U.S. exports to Japan are up 50% since 1987; imports from Japan are up 10%.

- Japan spends $30 billion a year on its Self-Defense Force, one of the world's largest military budgets.

- The U.S. has 56,000 troops in Japan. Japan pays 72% of the nonsalary cost of support.

BACKGROUND

Since the end of World War II, Japan and the U.S. have enjoyed a special relationship, based on mutual economic and political interests and a rapport that seemed to belie large differences between their two cultures. This friendship, which the late Ambassador Mike Mansfield characterized as "the most important bilateral relationship in the world," was bolstered by the realities of the cold war. The Communist takeover of China in 1949, the outbreak of the Korean War in 1950, and the presence of a hostile Soviet Union across the Sea of Japan strengthened Tokyo's alliance with Washington. Under that alliance, Japan prospered. Prevented by its own constitution from making war and protected by the U.S. from attack, Japan, helped initially by massive American aid, became an economic giant.

■ **INVESTMENT AND TRADE:** As Japan's prosperity grew, Americans looked to Japan for investment capital and markets for U.S. exports. By the end of the 1980s, 33 of the 50 states had trade offices in Tokyo. Indiana, Ohio,

Kentucky and other states have granted millions of dollars in subsidies and tax incentives to attract Japanese investments. Japan is now the second-largest foreign investor in the U.S., behind Britain, with investments of $300 billion. But British ownership of American industry grew slowly over two centuries, while Japan's surged in the 1980s as the country looked for opportunities to invest its growing wealth.

As U.S.-Japanese economic relations grew, so did friction. During the 1980s, Americans accused the Japanese of "dumping" their products in the U.S., charging unfairly low prices in order to undercut domestic competitors and increase their market share. Many U.S. exporters charged that Japanese distribution practices discriminated against imports and an "old boy" network of business and government alliances conspired to undermine foreign businesses. At the same time, Japan's American critics were concerned that Japanese were gaining undue political and economic influence in U.S. domestic affairs as a result of this country's growing dependence on Japanese capital to finance government debt and Japanese investment to spur industrial growth.

Japanese attribute their success to the superior quality of their products, a disciplined labor force that works longer hours than American workers, and a high savings rate—not unfair business practices. The economic problems of the U.S., they say, are largely of its own making, brought on by greed and undisciplined spending that has fueled skyrocketing U.S. government, corporate and personal debt.

While there is distrust and disillusionment with the U.S., Japanese still regard America as their closest—and perhaps only—true friend in the world. Similarly, some 77% of Americans, according to an opinion poll conducted by *The New York Times,* have friendly feelings toward Japan. Even many so-called Japan-bashers insist that they respect the Japanese and do not want to undermine the alliance. Yet disagreement persists over how to iron out the problems.

ECONOMIC RELATIONS

■ **PROTECTIONISM:** The persistent trade imbalance with Japan and U.S. difficulties penetrating the Japanese market have provoked a rise in protectionist legislation. In 1991 and again in 1992, House majority leader Richard A. Gephardt (D-Mo.), a leading critic of Japanese trade practices, proposed legislation curtailing U.S. imports of Japanese autos unless Japan cuts its trade surplus with the U.S. by 20% a year over the next five years. The move would slash annual Japanese car sales in the U.S. by 250,000. Although such protectionist measures are backed by U.S. auto industry leaders and labor unions, critics believe the legislation would actually hurt Americans.

Japanese automakers have invested roughly $9 billion in their U.S. automobile plants, helping to create more than 110,000 American jobs. Opponents of protectionism maintain that heavy foreign investment is a sign of U.S. economic strength because it demonstrates the appeal of America's political stability and skilled labor force. Moreover, they note, the lines between foreign and domestic have blurred in the modern global economy.

In Jan. 1992, President George Bush went on a 10-day tour of Australia and Asia. In an effort to silence critics who charged that his free-trade policies were in part responsible for a persistent recession, Bush proclaimed that his visit to Tokyo was primarily about "jobs." The President was accompanied by the chairmen of the "Big Three" U.S. automakers—General Motors, Ford and Chrysler. (Automobiles and auto parts accounted for 62% of the trade deficit with Japan in 1991.) The President became ill and collapsed during a state dinner with Japanese Prime Minister Kiichi Miyazawa. Many observers characterized the visit as a disaster. Free-traders felt the President had undermined his own policy. Others called the trade concessions he obtained from Tokyo inconsequential.

Japan's five largest automakers gave President Bush a pledge in Jan. to double to nearly $20 billion the value of imports of American-made auto parts by 1995. They also

Danziger. The Christian Science Monitor © 1992 TCSPS

agreed to step up efforts to distribute U.S.-made automobiles. In March, Tokyo's Ministry of International Trade and Industry announced that Japan would lower its "voluntary" limits on car exports to the U.S. for fiscal year 1992 to 1.7 million from the current 2.3 million. The reduction is not expected to make much of an impact on auto exports to the U.S., according to some analysts, because Japanese automakers have been stepping up production at their U.S. plants.

In May, the Japanese government issued an international trade policy statement in which it criticized protectionists in the U.S. but also acknowledged a need to open wider its markets to foreign business and pledged to promote global free trade. Many Japanese are dismayed that trade has become a U.S. election issue and would rather have Tokyo offer trade concessions than risk damaging the alliance.

Gov. Bill Clinton of Arkansas, the front-runner in the race for the Democratic presidential nomination, and H. Ross Perot, a billionaire businessman mounting an independent race for the White House, have said they see domestic failings rather than unfair foreign competition as the main source of U.S. trade problems. (See Chapter 3.) Neither has endorsed protectionist policies.

■ **U.S. PUBLIC OPINION POLLS** reflect ambivalence over protectionism. A Jan. 1992 survey by Marttila & Kiley and the *Detroit Free Press* showed that some 59% of those polled favored more restrictions on the sale of Japanese products in the U.S., even if it meant paying higher prices for domestic goods. Yet the same poll also found that 67% of the respondents agreed that Americans are too inclined to blame Japan for the country's economic difficulties.

Most respondents in another survey, by the Council on Competitiveness, said they believed Japan now makes better cars than America and faulted U.S. auto executives for concentrating on short-term profits instead of long-term gain.

■ **JAPANESE INVESTMENT:** During the 1980s, capital from Japan and West Germany fueled America's economic expansion. Today both economic giants are weakening. Germany is in the costly process of absorbing the former East Germany, and Japan has its own economic headaches.

Many Americans who once feared an invasion of Japanese capital now worry that it may be withdrawn. Foreign investment (primarily Japanese) in the U.S. declined from a peak of $166.9 billion in 1987 to $11.8 billion in 1991. Tokyo's stock market crash was the main reason for the slowdown, analysts say. The Nikkei index has dived more than 50% from its record high of 38,915 in Dec. 1989 to 16,598 in April 1992. Many Japanese banks are heavily invested in stocks. As stock prices decline, Japanese banks and corporations are cutting back loans and investments overseas.

Other analysts do not believe that Japan's economic troubles will undermine the U.S. They maintain that the Japanese hold less than 2% of total U.S. government obligations and that, as the world's biggest and safest economic power, the U.S. can attract all the capital it needs to finance the budget deficit and private investment, even if the price will be higher interest rates.

DIPLOMATIC/SECURITY RELATIONS

The U.S. has called on Japan to abandon its inward-looking approach for a more active role in international affairs. This comes at a time of uncertainty over the future of the U.S. military role in Asian security. If the U.S. were to disengage from Asia, some analysts believe it would create a power vacuum that would force Tokyo to expand its defenses to protect its economic interests. That prospect troubles South Korea, the Philippines, China and other Asian countries with bitter memories of Japanese occupation during World War II. A strong U.S. presence reassures Japan's neighbors that Japanese militarism will not reassert itself.

When Iraqi President Saddam Hussein invaded Kuwait in Aug. 1990, President Bush and Japanese Prime Minister Toshiki Kaifu closely coordinated their responses. However, bickering over Japan's economic contribution to the U.S.-led coalition clouded the alliance. In the end, Japan contributed $13 billion. Washington also wanted Japan to send nonmilitary personnel to the region, but Tokyo refused, demonstrating an increasingly independent spirit. (In Japan, the Gulf crisis touched off a debate over the once-taboo subject of sending troops overseas.

COMING SOON!

Oliver Stone!!!'s

GHWB

The Story That Won't Go Home

OLIVER STONE'S LATEST CONSPIRACY THEORY ON WHAT HAPPENED IN TOKYO LAST WEEK STARRING LEE IACOCCA, RICHARD GEPHARDT, MARILYN QUAYLE, JOHN SUNUNU, MICHAEL DUKAKIS, BOB DOLE, AND A DESPONDENT SUSHI CHEF under the control of Ramsey Clark.

also starring Kevin Costner as the Trade Deficit

R RESTRICTED
UNDER 17 REQUIRES ACCOMPANYING
PARENT OR ADULT GUARDIAN

DANZIGER

Danziger. The Christian Science Monitor © 1992 TCSPS

In June 1992, the Japanese parliament approved a bill permitting Japan to play a limited role in international peacekeeping operations.)

The question of Japanese aid for, among others, the former Soviet republics is another source of continuing friction between Washington and Tokyo. The U.S., not to mention Germany and France, would like Japan to provide substantial aid to help convert the republics to market economies. Japan insists that the issue of the "Northern Islands" must be settled first. (In the final days of World War II, the Soviet Union seized four islands in the Kurile chain which Tokyo claims belong to Japan.) Japan did agree in May 1992 to provide loans totaling as much as $400 million to spur private enterprise in Eastern and Central Europe. The announcement came at the end of a visit to Japan by Vice President Dan Quayle.

The U.S. insistence on Japan's increasing its aid efforts has prompted some Japanese to complain that the so-called global partnership means Japanese dollars and U.S. leadership.

ADMINISTRATION POLICY

■ **TRADE AND ECONOMIC RELATIONS:** The White House acknowledges a need for Japan to open further its markets but takes the position that intensive negotiations with Tokyo have paid off in reduced trade barriers and a rise in U.S. exports. At the same time, the White House has not hesitated to retaliate against what it sees as unfair trade practices. In 1989 it cited Japan, under Section 301 of the Omnibus Trade and Competitiveness Act, for blocking sales of supercomputers, satellites and wood products. The so-called Super 301 calls for retaliation against countries deemed to be unfair traders through the imposition of import quotas and tariffs. (Critics charge that Super 301 violates GATT.) In April 1990, Bush removed the unfair trader label, prompting hope that the Japanese would open their markets further.

■ **POLITICAL RELATIONS:** The Administration maintains that an "increasingly active, engaged and responsible Japan is crucial to the post-cold-war world." Washington and Tokyo, which contribute 40% of all bilateral aid, support a new global partnership to help countries that are in transition to democracy and market economies. The U.S. has asked Tokyo to increase its efforts to promote economic growth and political stability in the developing world. It calls for a continuation of the U.S.-Japan alliance to bolster military security in Asia.

POLICY CHOICES

1. THE U.S. SHOULD PUT GREATER PRESSURE ON JAPAN TO OPEN ITS MARKETS.

YES. The U.S. must be prepared to place additional restrictions on trade with Japan and review its defense commitment unless Japan gives the U.S. greater access to its markets. This should be part of a new economic strategy to cope with the challenges posed by "managed trade" economies.

NO. The Super 301 provision and the bilateral negotiations have resulted in lowering trade barriers. No additional pressure is needed: it would only damage the special relationship and encourage Tokyo to forge other economic alliances.

2. THE U.S. SHOULD URGE JAPAN TO PLAY A MORE ACTIVE INTERNATIONAL ROLE.

YES. The U.S. should adapt to the post-cold-war world by building a new collaborative, power-sharing effort with Japan. Japan in turn should assume a larger international role commensurate with its position as a leading economic power.

NO. Encouraging Japan to play a larger political and military role would produce a backlash among its neighbors who still bear battle scars from World War II. Furthermore, such pressure could produce an isolationist, anti-American reaction in Japan.

SELECT BIBLIOGRAPHY

Baker, Howard H., Jr., and Frost, Ellen L., "Rescuing the U.S.-Japan Alliance." *Foreign Affairs,* Spring 1992, pp. 97–113. Basing their findings on a Council on Foreign Relations study group headed by Mr. Baker, the authors urge both nations to accept their differences as they work out a new global agenda.

Funabashi, Yoichi, "Japan and America: Global Partners." *Foreign Policy,* Spring 1992, pp. 24–39. The author, a distinguished Japanese diplomatic correspondent, examines the pitfalls and potential of relations between Tokyo and Washington.

"Japanese-U.S. Trade: Harmony or Discord?" *Great Decisions 1991,* pp. 51–60. New York, Foreign Policy Association, 1991.

Reischauer, Edwin O., *The Japanese Today: Change and Continuity.* Cambridge, Mass., Belknap Press of Harvard University Press, 1988. A noted American scholar examines Japan's recent history, current tensions and future prospects.

US Department of State Dispatch, Jan. 20, 1992, pp. 35–50. Official statements by Washington and Tokyo following President Bush's visit to Japan.

5

Soviet Breakup: U.S. Policy Dilemmas

✔ *Should the U.S. develop a new 'Marshall Plan' to help the nations of the former Soviet Union become free-market democracies?*

✔ *How much aid should America provide?*

✔ *What can Washington do to prevent the spread of Russian nuclear weapons and technology?*

BASIC FACTS

■ **U.S.S.R.,** with a population of 290 million and stretching across 11 time zones, ceased to exist Dec. 25, 1991.

■ Former U.S.S.R. split into 15 countries: 3 Baltic states (Estonia, Latvia and Lithuania), Georgia and 11 former republics loosely associated in the **Commonwealth of Independent States (CIS).**

■ CIS includes:

  Slavic republics (made up 70% of population and contained 80% of industry of former U.S.S.R.):

  —Russian Federation: 147 million people and largest, most powerful of former Soviet republics.

  —Ukraine: 52 million people, size of France in population and area and CIS's second most powerful state.

  —Belarus (formerly Byelorussia): 10.3 million people; site of Chernobyl.

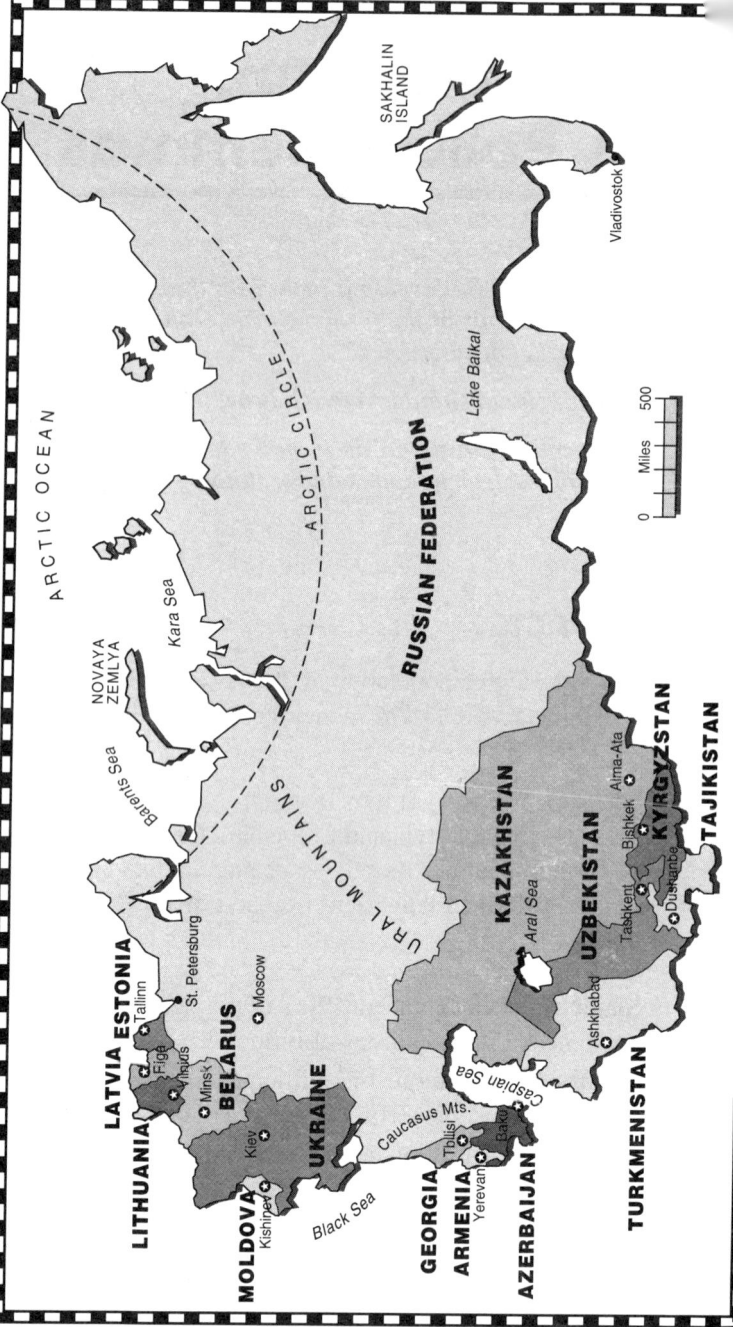

ARCTIC OCEAN

NOVAYA
ZEMLYA

Kara Sea

Barents Sea

ARCTIC CIRCLE

SAKHALIN
ISLAND

Vladivostok

RUSSIAN FEDERATION

Lake Baikal

URAL MOUNTAINS

0   Miles   500

LATVIA ESTONIA

Tallinn

St. Petersburg

Moscow

Riga

Vilnius

LITHUANIA

Minsk

BELARUS

MOLDOVA

Kiev

Kishinev

UKRAINE

Black Sea

Caucasus Mts.

GEORGIA

Tbilisi

ARMENIA

Yerevan

AZERBAIJAN

Baku

Caspian Sea

TURKMENISTAN

Ashkhabad

Aral Sea

KAZAKHSTAN

UZBEKISTAN

Tashkent

Alma-Ata

Bishkek

KYRGYZSTAN

Dushanbe

TAJIKISTAN

Muslim republics of Central Asia (comprise one third of Asia, from Caspian Sea to China):

—Kazakhstan: 17 million people, in a nation the size of India; rich in oil, coal, other minerals.

—Uzbekistan: 20 million people in area larger than California.

—Turkmenistan: 3.6 million people; cotton, some oil and gas.

—Tajikistan: 5.1 million people; cattle and sheep raising.

—Kyrgyzstan: 4.3 million people; wool and live-stock producing.

Caucasus republics:

—Armenia: 3.5 million people; smallest former republic.

—Azerbaijan: 7 million people;oil, iron industries.

[Georgia, with 5.5 million people, has not joined CIS.]

Moldova (formerly Moldavia): 4.4 million people; part of Romania until it was seized by Stalin in 1940.

■ **Economic aid**

• Total aid to U.S.S.R. and its successor-states between Sept. 1990 and Dec. 1991: $80 billion.

• Group of Seven (G-7) leading industrial nations announced $24 billion, one-year aid program for Russia on April 1, 1992; includes proposed U.S. contribution of nearly $4.5 billion.

• Estimated need: International Monetary Fund (IMF) estimates that 15 former republics will need $100 billion over the next four years.

■ **Nuclear weapons:** over 25,000 warheads, located in Russia, Ukraine, Belarus and Kazakhstan, which are under Russian control.

BACKGROUND

When President Mikhail S. Gorbachev came to power in 1985, the Soviet Union faced severe social and economic problems, including bureaucratic inefficiency and corruption, a lack of fundamental freedoms, and a centralized planning system that produced severe shortages and shoddy goods. Military spending had helped sap the economy. Industrial regions were fouled by pollution. Harvests rotted in the fields because a primitive infrastructure prevented adequate food distribution. The standard of living was falling. Even average life expectancy had declined.

Gorbachev introduced *perestroika*—a program to restructure the economy by easing the state's control—and *glasnost,* a policy of greater political openness. The first made living conditions worse; the second weakened the Kremlin's tight rein on the political process. The Soviet republics agitated increasingly for greater independence from Moscow's control. By Aug. 1991, in a compromise effort to hold the country together, Gorbachev had forged a new Treaty of Union that would have granted the republics greater autonomy. But on Aug. 19, a few days before the treaty was to be signed, hard-line Communists launched a coup. Their effort to wrest power from Gorbachev failed as the military refused to open fire on demonstrators in Moscow and Leningrad. The coup attempt discredited the Communist party, destroyed the union treaty, and accelerated the Soviet Union's breakup. One after another, the republics declared independence. The Kremlin's fate was sealed on Dec. 1, 1991, when Ukrainians, almost one fifth of the country's population, voted to form their own nation.

As Gorbachev's hold on power weakened, Russian President Boris N. Yeltsin's influence grew. Yeltsin had been elected president in June 1991 in the first free, multiparty popular election in Russian history. On Dec. 8, 1991, Russia, Ukraine and Belarus agreed to form the Commonwealth of Independent States. By Dec. 21, the

SOME ASSEMBLY REQUIRED

HENRY PAYNE. Reprinted by permission of UFS, Inc.

CIS had expanded to include all the former Soviet republics except the three Baltic states and Georgia, which was torn by civil war. On Dec. 25, Gorbachev declared that the Soviet Union had ceased to exist. Although communism was discredited, former Communist leaders still exercise political control in former republics such as Kazakhstan, Uzbekistan and Azerbaijan.

■ **THE PROBLEMS AHEAD:** The CIS is a commonwealth in name only. The countries it comprises are wracked by ethnic tension and economic uncertainty. Although CIS members have declared that they will cooperate on defense, economic reform and other issues, consensus will be difficult to achieve. Territorial disputes have already brought Azerbaijan and Armenia into open warfare. The historic antipathy between Russia and Ukraine is complicated by new rivalries. Moscow, for example, wants to keep a single, unified, supranational armed force encompassing a "common strategic space," but Ukraine wants its own armed forces. The two nations also disagree over the Black Sea fleet, based in the Ukrainian city of Sevastopol. Ukraine claims many of the ships; Russia insists they should be under CIS control.

■ **ECONOMIC REFORMS:** In Russia, Yeltsin has speeded

the pace of free-market reforms, including the sale of state enterprises and the ending of price controls. As a result, hundreds of thousands lost their jobs, production fell, inflation soared, hoarding grew and goods disappeared from the marketplace. Food, housing and heating fuel are more expensive and in short supply. So are medical supplies. Analysts warned that 1992 would be worse than 1991. As conditions deteriorated, Yeltsin and leaders of other republics pressed for Western help.

■ **WESTERN AID:** At a summit of the G-7 nations in London in July 1991, the U.S., Britain and Japan turned down an appeal by Gorbachev for $20 billion to $30 billion of Western capital, saying that the money would be wasted unless the Kremlin first embraced a free-market economy. Nevertheless, the G-7, which also includes Canada, France, Germany and Italy, agreed to provide technical assistance, including advice about converting Soviet industry from military to civilian use and improving food distribution. At the same time, President George Bush approved $1.5 billion in agricultural loan guarantees for the Soviets. This was in addition to an earlier loan of $1 billion he had approved in Dec. 1990. The Administration indicated that further aid would be on a step-by-step basis as reforms were implemented.

After the Aug. 1991 coup by hard-line Communists, which failed to overthrow Gorbachev, German Chancellor Helmut Kohl urged the U.S. and Japan to increase their aid. (Since 1989, Germany has committed more than $45 billion, over half of all Western aid to the former Soviet Union. Much of the German aid is part of an agreement providing for the withdrawal of Soviet troops from the former East Germany and covers the cost of housing for the returning troops.)

As Yeltsin pushed ahead with the free-market reforms that Gorbachev had avoided, he pressed harder for Western aid. In Jan. 1992, the Administration announced it would begin airlifting food and medical supplies in Feb., adding approximately $645 million to the $1.4 billion in food aid it had announced the previous Nov. Since 1989, the U.S. has spent roughly $4.6 billion in assisting the former Soviet Union.

■ **AID DEBATE:** While few dispute that political and economic instability, especially in those republics with access to nuclear weaponry, would pose a serious threat, there is disagreement over what kind and how much aid to provide, especially at a time when the U.S. is faced with a huge national debt, a federal budget deficit, troubling social problems and a recession that has left 9 million Americans jobless.

Former President Richard M. Nixon, in a memo made public in March, called U.S. aid efforts "a pathetically inadequate response." He added: "The Communists have lost the cold war, but the West has not yet won it." If Yeltsin's reforms fail, Nixon warned, "war could break out in the former Soviet Union.... The new East European democracies would be imperiled."

Many Democrats and Republicans, among them Democratic presidential aspirant Bill Clinton, governor of Arkansas, criticized Bush's hesitancy to provide more funds to the Soviets. "The President kept America largely on the sidelines in the democratic revolution that toppled the Soviet empire and is transforming the face of world politics," Clinton said in a speech to the Foreign Policy Association on April 1. Stating that "the revolution must not fail," Clinton called for foreign aid for a democratic Russia, which he called a "short-term investment in our long-term security." Clinton joined Nixon in urging the Administration to do more. Coincidentally with the Clinton speech, President Bush, joined by Chancellor Helmut Kohl, on April 1 unveiled a G-7 $24 billion aid program. The program includes a $6 billion stabilization fund to maintain the value of the ruble by giving the government the ability to intervene in currency markets when the ruble falls below a certain value; $11 billion in export and grain credits; $4.5 billion in loans from the IMF, the World Bank and other institutions; and a $2.5 billion deferral of Russian debts. To get the aid, Russia, which became a member of the IMF in June, must follow an IMF-approved economic reform program. Other former Soviet republics must do likewise if they are to get similar assistance.

Some have called for the U.S. to institute a new Marshall Plan, based on the massive U.S. relief effort to help Europe recover from the devastation of World War II. "If aid helps Mr. Yeltsin's government to resist its opponents and carry its program through, it will be money well spent," *The Economist* (London), editorialized in April. "Let the West be clear, the difficulties of this undertaking are so formidable that the chances of success can be no better than 50–50. But until recently it was impossible to study Russia without concluding that economic catastrophe was certain. Now a remarkable change has taken place. Remembering the stakes, it makes the gamble worth taking."

Others favor continuing humanitarian support and modest technical assistance, but argue that the U.S. is too strapped for cash to promise much. Many liberal Democrats argue that the White House should not talk of sending money abroad when domestic racial and economic problems boil over at home, as they did in May in Los Angeles with widespread rioting and looting.

Some conservatives in Congress argue that aid will simply strengthen a historical adversary who may become hostile again. Others maintain that the former Soviet Union's problems are so enormous that no amount of aid will help, and whatever is provided will be wasted. Some observers maintain that the former Soviet states can best be helped by encouraging private trade and investment. For example, Robert L. Bartley, editor of *The Wall Street Journal,* doubts that aid will do much good. He maintains that if Russia acts forcibly to ensure property rights and enforce contracts, "capitalism will happen."

■ **NUCLEAR PROLIFERATION:** The U.S. and other nations are concerned about the fate of the former Soviet Union's

25,000 nuclear warheads, including almost 11,000 strategic warheads. The CIS member-states agreed in Dec. 1991 that nuclear forces would remain under a unified command dominated by Russia. Russia has 70% of the weapons; the rest are in Ukraine, Kazakhstan and Belarus. In May 1992 Kazakhstan joined Ukraine and Belarus in declaring its intention to be a nonnuclear state. Kazakhstan's leader, President Nursultan Nazarbayev, had initially balked at giving up the nuclear weapons, citing political uncertainty in Russia and the fact that neighboring China is continuing its nuclear tests. Kazakhstan's decision cleared the way for the U.S., Russia and the other states of the former Soviet Union to put the decade-old strategic arms reduction treaty (Start) into effect. Under that agreement, signed by Bush and Gorbachev in July 1991, the two superpowers agreed to cut their strategic nuclear arsenals by about 30% within seven years. (See Chapter 2.) The former Soviet states also agreed to sign and abide by the 1968 Nuclear Nonproliferation Treaty and to permit international inspections of nuclear installations within their borders.

Many analysts worry that controlling the vast array of nuclear material, technology and expertise will grow increasingly difficult. Nuclear technology and the materials to develop it might be sold to unstable Third World governments such as Iraq or Iran or to radical fringe groups who might use them for political blackmail. Therefore, they believe the U.S. should make safeguarding these weapons a defense priority, and support using U.S. defense funds to help the former Soviets destroy them. In Nov. 1991, Rep. Les Aspin (D-Wis.) and Sen. Sam Nunn (D-Ga.) proposed using $1 billion in defense funds to help with dismantling nuclear, chemical and biological weapons and to deliver food and medicine. The Administration opposed the measure. On Nov. 25, the Senate overwhelmingly approved spending up to $500 million of Defense Department funds: $400 million for assistance with the destruction and safeguarding of weapons and $100 million for transportation of humanitarian aid.

ADMINISTRATION POLICY

■ **AID:** In his initial response to Nixon's criticism, President Bush declared that his Administration did not have a "blank check" to finance extensive aid programs. The U.S. has now pledged $1.5 billion to the $6 billion ruble stabilization fund, $850 million in other loans, and about $2 billion in aid. Bush has also said he will seek congressional authorization to funnel as much as $15 billion to international lending institutions for interest-bearing loans to the former republics.

The Administration says America's more than $4 billion contribution to the G-7 plan will come from previously collected funds, not new taxes. Responding to critics who say the U.S. cannot afford such expenditures, Bush argues that "we have an enormous stake, a personal stake for every American, in the success of these democracies....To risk their failure by doing nothing is very short-sighted...."

Nations that pursue reforms, move significantly toward democracy and a market economy and respect human rights are more likely to gain foreign aid. If chaos reigns, the prospects for foreign aid are less likely.

■ **NUCLEAR WEAPONS:** The White House has urged the former Soviet republics to cooperate in maintaining safe command and control of nuclear weapons. In return for President Nazarbayev's pledge in May 1992 to eliminate the nuclear missiles deployed in Kazakhstan, the U.S. agreed to provide federal loan guarantees for American businesses locating in Kazakhstan and promised to lower trade barriers and encourage investment. The U.S. is negotiating with Russia reductions in the nuclear giants' arsenals that go well beyond the limits agreed to in Start.

POLICY CHOICES

1. THE U.S. SHOULD INCREASE AID TO RUSSIA AND THE OTHER REPUBLICS.

YES. (1) Substantial U.S. aid and technical assistance are necessary if ambitious free-market reforms are to be successful. (2) A more stable economic climate resulting from the reforms will pay off in the long run by opening up new markets for U.S. exports. (3) Stability in the former Soviet Union will reduce risks of war and lessen the U.S. defense burden.

NO. (1) More American economic aid now would be wasted: the former Soviet republics are not using the foreign capital they now have effectively. (2) A new economic system cannot be imposed from the outside. (3) U.S. economic intervention could be seriously destabilizing, touching off a xenophobic reaction.

2. THE U.S. SHOULD REDUCE ITS NUCLEAR STOCKPILE BEYOND THE START LIMITS.

YES. The former Soviet Union no longer poses a military threat to the U.S. Therefore the U.S. can proceed to reduce its stockpile beyond Start goals—to 500–1,000 warheads—without risk.

NO. No further cuts should be made until all nuclear weapons are on Russian soil and in Russian custody and there are adequate safeguards that Russia will not disseminate nuclear weapons technology or the weapons themselves.

SELECT BIBLIOGRAPHY

"Breakup of the Soviet Union: U.S. Dilemma." *Great Decisions 1992*, pp. 81–90. New York, Foreign Policy Association, 1992. A nonpartisan look at differing views on how the U.S. should approach aid and security issues with the new nations of the former Soviet Union.

Bush, George, "Efforts to Aid New Independent States at 'Defining Moment in History.' " *US Department of State Dispatch*, April 6, 1992, pp. 261–66. White House statements on the Administration's proposals to aid the new nations of the former Soviet Union. April 1, 1992.

Lynch, Allen, "The Soviet Breakup and U.S. Foreign Policy." *Headline Series* No. 297. New York, Foreign Policy Association, Summer 1992. Thorough background on the last years of the Soviet superpower and the nations that replaced it.

One Nation Becomes Many: The Access Guide to the Former Soviet Union. ACCESS, 1730 M St., N.W., Suite 605, Washington, D.C. 20036, 1992. A comprehensive guide to the issues and options facing U.S. policymakers, published by the nonprofit, nonpartisan clearinghouse of information on international security, peace and world affairs.

Policy and the Disintegration of the U.S.S.R. New York, Council on Foreign Relations, 1991. Five eminent Sovietologists examine what brought the Soviet Union to its knees and assess what is likely to happen next.

6

U.S. Foreign Aid

✔ *Is foreign aid necessary to promote U.S. foreign policy goals?*

✔ *What strings, if any, should be tied to foreign aid?*

✔ *Should the U.S. restore funding for the UN population program?*

BASIC FACTS

- **Foreign aid budget** for fiscal year (FY) 1992: $14.2 billion. FY1991: $15.4 billion.

- **Major recipients:** Israel, $3 billion; Egypt, $2.3 billion; Turkey, Greece and Portugal (NATO allies), $1.2 billion; Andean nations (Bolivia, Colombia, Ecuador and Peru), $597 million; Philippines, $557 million; Eastern Europe, $400 million.

  [For U.S. aid and credits to Russia and other former Soviet republics, see Chapter 5.]

- **Foreign aid as % of federal budget:** less than 1%.

- Percentage of U.S. gross national product (GNP) spent on foreign aid: 0.15%. U.S. contributes smallest percentage of GNP of the 18 leading industrial countries.

BACKGROUND

Foreign aid has played a key role in promoting U.S. foreign policy goals since World War II. The single largest U.S. foreign aid program was the Marshall Plan (1948–

FY 1992 Economic, Development, and Humanitarian Assistance: $11.1 billion*

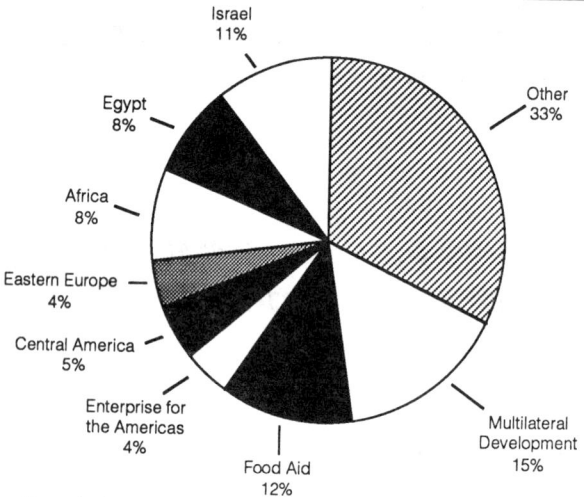

Israel
11%

Egypt
8%

Africa
8%

Eastern Europe
4%

Central America
5%

Enterprise for
the Americas
4%

Food Aid
12%

Other
33%

Multilateral
Development
15%

* Discretionary budget authority.

Note: Food aid provides additional assistance to countries and regions identified separately. Eastern Europe includes $70 million for the European Bank for Reconstruction and Development.

52): the U.S. contributed $13.3 billion to rebuild Europe. Since the mid-1950s, most foreign aid has gone to developing countries.

U.S. foreign aid policy developed within the context of the cold war. Its primary focus was containing Soviet influence and safeguarding U.S. security, but it has had many other complex goals: providing humanitarian relief from famine, war and natural disasters; promoting development through technical assistance, education, investment, family planning, disease prevention, etc.; and creating markets for U.S. farmers and business.

■ **FOREIGN AID BREAKDOWN:** The U.S. provides several types of aid:
  ■ **Security assistance** aims to increase the stability of nations of strategic and political importance to the U.S. It has traditionally comprised the bulk of U.S. foreign aid, and most of it has gone to the wealthier

FY 1992 International Affairs Appropriations Request

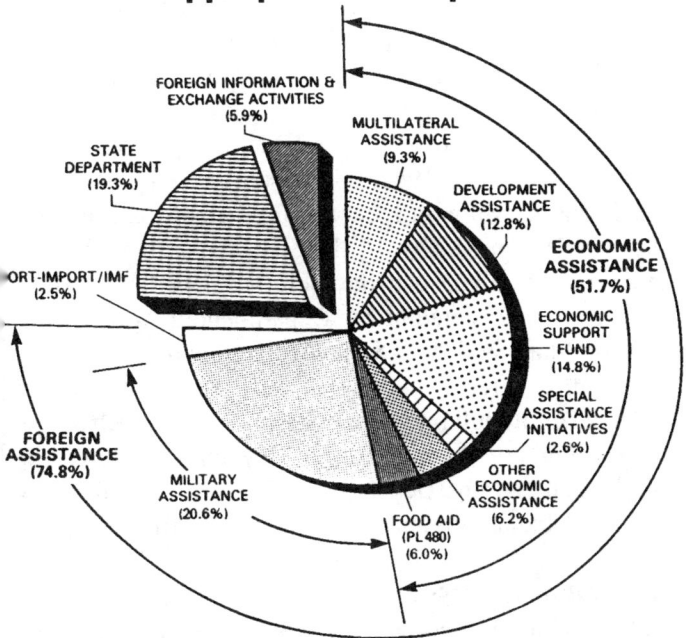

FOREIGN INFORMATION & EXCHANGE ACTIVITIES
(5.9%)

STATE DEPARTMENT
(19.3%)

ORT-IMPORT/IMF
(2.5%)

MULTILATERAL ASSISTANCE
(9.3%)

DEVELOPMENT ASSISTANCE
(12.8%)

ECONOMIC ASSISTANCE
(51.7%)

ECONOMIC SUPPORT FUND
(14.8%)

SPECIAL ASSISTANCE INITIATIVES
(2.6%)

OTHER ECONOMIC ASSISTANCE
(6.2%)

FOREIGN ASSISTANCE
(74.8%)

MILITARY ASSISTANCE
(20.6%)

FOOD AID (PL 480)
(6.0%)

nations in which the U.S. has a special interest rather than to the neediest. Security assistance has two components:

military aid, which includes grants and credits for defense materials, services and training, and compensation for the presence of U.S. military bases; and the

Economic Support Fund, which serves both economic and security goals; it can be used to buy commodities, for balance-of-payments support or as cash grants.

- **Development assistance** includes technical aid, loans and grants to promote long-term material progress and stability in the poorer nations.
- **Disaster assistance** includes emergency relief from famine, earthquakes and war.
- **Food aid (Food for Peace)** includes food given to developing countries for emergency and humanitar-

ian relief and to promote economic development. About 70% is given to very poor countries, the rest is sold for local currencies or dollars on credit terms. Food aid is provided through the Agricultural Trade Development and Assistance Act of 1954, known as PL 480.

The U.S. Agency for International Development (AID), founded in 1961, administers development aid, the Economic Support Fund and food grants; military assistance is administered by the State Department in consultation with AID and the Defense Department; food sales are administered by the Department of Agriculture.

More than 80% of U.S. development aid is dispensed bilaterally—directly to recipient nations. The balance is channeled through multilateral organizations, such as the World Bank, the Inter-American Development Bank and the United Nations Development Program, and through private voluntary organizations such as CARE.

■ **PUBLIC ATTITUDES:** Misconceptions about foreign aid abound. A poll cited by *U.S. News & World Report* in Feb. 1992 found 70% of respondents believed 10% or more of the federal budget was spent on foreign aid; nearly half believed the percentage was at least 25%. The actual figure is closer to 1%.

■ **BUDGET:** The Bush Administration sought $15.3 billion for foreign aid in FY 1992, compared with $15.4 billion appropriated in 1991. After many delays caused by disagreements between Congress and the White House, Congress on March 31–April 1, 1992 (the last possible moment) approved a continuing resolution to fund foreign aid through Sept. 30, the end of the fiscal year. The final budget signed by the President on April 1 was for $14.2 billion, $1.2 billion less than for FY 1991.

■ **HELPING THE FORMER SOVIET REPUBLICS AND ISRAEL:** A major issue in the 1991–92 foreign aid debate was support for the former Soviet republics. In late 1991 Con-

Swann—The Huntsville Times, AL. ROTHCO

gress appropriated $500 million, drawn from Defense
Department funds, to finance the destruction of nuclear
weapons and transport humanitarian relief supplies. In
Jan. President Bush promised to provide $645 million in
new funds for humanitarian and technical aid. In April,
amid rising pressure to help the republics, Bush announced he would ask Congress to approve almost $4.5
billion as part of a $24 billion package assembled by the
seven major industrial countries to help Russia. The
President asked Congress to act promptly to approve the
measure. (See Chapter 5.)

Another controversial issue in the foreign aid debate
was Israel's request for $10 billion in loan guarantees
over five years to help absorb and house Jewish immi-
grants from the former Soviet Union and Ethiopia. Bush
refused unless Israel agreed to a total freeze in building
Jewish settlements in the occupied West Bank and Gaza
Strip. (See Chapter 7.) After the White House threatened
to veto the foreign aid bill, the House took no action and
the Senate passed a nonbinding resolution expressing
support for "appropriate loan guarantees" by a vote of
99–1.

■ **FAMILY PLANNING:** The U.S. has traditionally played a

key role in promoting family planning and helped establish the UN Population Fund (Unfpa), the world's largest intergovernmental family-planning organization, which helps developing nations address the problems associated with rapid population growth. In the mid-1980s, the Reagan Administration suspended funding for Unfpa because it provided funds to China, which allegedly used coercive family-planning practices such as forced abortions. Many lawmakers favor refunding the program, while the Administration continues to oppose it. House attempts to reintroduce Unfpa funding in the 1992 foreign aid authorization bill were partially responsible for a threatened presidential veto and the subsequent death of the authorization legislation.

■ **REFORM:** Pressure to reform foreign aid priorities and practices has been building from quarters ranging from AID to academia to Congress. The 1961 Foreign Assistance Act is the main legislation that guides U.S. foreign aid. In 1973 it was revised with the "New Directions" initiative, which increased congressional control over spending and gave priority to meeting the basic needs of the world's poor over promoting self-sustaining economic growth.

In early 1989, a special task force of the House Foreign Affairs Committee proposed overhauling foreign aid legislation, refocusing objectives, reducing restrictions, improving accountability by recipients and giving the President more say in managing foreign aid. A self-critical AID assessment the same year found foreign aid was perpetuating instead of reducing poor countries' dependence. Congressional and White House attempts to implement some of the task force recommendations in 1990 and 1991 failed.

The congressional practice of earmarking a significant portion of bilateral aid for specific programs and countries is particularly controversial. The Administration objects that earmarking limits its flexibility to respond to U.S. interests and new developments. Congress rebuts

hat it is the only way to guarantee funding for programs
he executive branch might otherwise ignore.

A major issue facing Congress and the Administration
s how to fund foreign aid amid falling public support and
rising demands, especially from Eastern Europe and the
former Soviet republics. Speaking of foreign aid, Democratic presidential candidate Gov. Bill Clinton of Arkansas stated that "it is deeply irresponsible to forgo this
short-term investment in our long-term security." In the
long run, it could cost the country more in higher defense
budgets and lost economic opportunities.

Some critics of current foreign aid policy would cut
aid to wealthier nations such as Israel and Egypt and funnel it instead to Africa and Eastern Europe. (Israel and
Egypt have received roughly 30% of foreign aid since the
signing of the 1979 Camp David accords.) One strategy
gaining support in the Administration and Congress is to
focus economic aid on programs that both promote economic development in poor countries and expand U.S. investment opportunities and markets. Supporters want to
tie more U.S. aid to the purchase of U.S. goods and to
target aid to capital or infrastructure projects requiring
materials from the U.S. Meanwhile, others question
whether food aid undermines farming in poor countries
and creates dependency, and wonder how to balance
feeding the world's hungry with providing outlets for surplus U.S. farm goods.

An alternative to foreign aid favored by some is freer
trade. According to an April 1992 World Bank report, a
50% reduction in trade barriers by the U.S., the European
Community and Japan would increase developing countries' exports by $50 billion a year, almost the equivalent
of the net flow of development aid in 1991.

Others point out that aid and trade should not be
viewed as alternatives but as complementary. According
to AID, U.S. exports to countries receiving U.S. assistance grew nearly 72% between 1985 and 1990. In 1991
more than 30% of U.S. exports were shipped to developing countries.

ADMINISTRATION POLICY

■ **BUDGET:** The Administration's foreign aid allocation. have changed little from previous years, with the follow ing exceptions: bilateral assistance to Eastern Europe anc the former Soviet Union in 1991 and 1992, and aid tc Nicaragua and Panama in 1990; increased financial sup- port for antidrug efforts in the Andean nations since 1990; and a five-fold increase in spending for environ- ment-related projects in recent years.

The U.S. has forgiven debts owed by Egypt and Po- land as well as by some African, Latin American and Caribbean nations.

■ **PRIORITIES:** The Administration considers foreign assis- tance "an essential tool in advancing U.S. interests in the 1990s." Its priorities, outlined in a statement of mission issued by AID in Sept. 1990, include promoting democ- racy, supporting free markets and broad-based economic growth, improving the economic and social well-being of individuals, encouraging the wise management of natural resources, protecting against transnational threats (drug trafficking, environmental degradation), and meeting emergency humanitarian needs. Funding priority is being given to nations that are implementing free-market and democratic reforms.

The Bush Administration has unveiled several new AID initiatives to support these goals. The **Democracy Initiative** seeks to establish mechanisms whereby AID can quickly assist nations moving toward democracy: it conditions funding on countries' efforts to support demo- cratic institutions and provides direct support for institu- tions such as electoral bodies and independent judiciaries. The **Partnership for Business and Development** initia- tive seeks to fund capital projects that can increase U.S. trade competitiveness in developing countries and en- courage U.S. investment. AID has also embarked on the most comprehensive reorganization of its structure and procedures since the 1970s.

POLICY CHOICES

1. THE U.S. SHOULD REDUCE OR ELIMINATE FOREIGN AID.

YES. The U.S. can no longer afford it; much of it is wasted; and it encourages dependence on the part of the recipients.

NO. About 70% of foreign aid is spent on U.S. goods and services; it creates markets for U.S. exports; and it provides the U.S. with leverage to promote its interests.

2. THE U.S. SHOULD ELIMINATE SECURITY ASSISTANCE.

YES. With the cold war over, the U.S. can redirect aid to relieving economic and social problems that threaten stability in the poorest developing nations.

NO. Although Soviet communism no longer poses a threat, some developing nations such as Iraq menace the peace, and their neighbors continue to look to the U.S. for assistance.

3. THE U.S. SHOULD TIE STRINGS ON AID.

YES. To qualify for aid, recipients must be prepared to implement free-market and democratic reforms, respect human rights and reduce military spending.

NO. Conditionality is desirable in principle, but it must be applied with discretion, avoiding the appearance that the U.S. is interfering in domestic affairs.

4. THE U.S. SHOULD CHANNEL MORE AID THROUGH MULTILATERAL AGENCIES.

YES. This would enable the U.S. to cut the size of its aid bureaucracy and reduce friction and misunderstandings between the U.S. and recipients.

NO. Dispensing aid directly gives the U.S. more leverage and ensures accountability on the part of recipients.

5. THE U.S. SHOULD RESTORE FUNDING TO THE UNFPA.

YES. Lack of U.S. financial support has decreased the availability of family-planning services and led to an increase, not a decrease, in abortions.

NO. According to AID, the U.S. provides 45% of all the family planning funds in the world. Current U.S. policy sends a signal to the world that abortion is not acceptable.

SELECT BIBLIOGRAPHY

Baker, James A., 3d, "FY 1993 Foreign Assistance Request—Partnership for Peace." *US Department of State Dispatch,* Feb. 24, 1992, pp. 121–25. In a statement before the House Foreign Operations Subcommittee, the secretary of state outlined his funding request for the former Soviet Union and other international needs.

Eberstadt, Nicholas, "U.S. Foreign Aid Policy—A Critique." *Headline Series* No. 293. New York, Foreign Policy Association, Summer 1990. The author makes recommendations for restoring what he considers the original purpose of U.S. foreign aid.

Nelson, Joan M., with Eglinton, Stephanie J., "Encouraging Democracy: What Role for Conditioned Aid?" *Policy Essay No. 4.* Washington, D.C., Overseas Development Council, 1992. Attaching conditions to aid may help promote human rights and democracy, but other avenues should be tried as well.

"Rethinking Foreign Aid: What Kind? How Much? For Whom?" *Great Decisions 1991,* pp. 43–50. New York, Foreign Policy Association, 1991. An overview of U.S. policy on foreign aid and alternative approaches.

7

The Middle East After the Gulf War

✔ *Should the U.S. maintain a military presence in the Middle East?*

✔ *Should the U.S. lean harder on Iraq to get rid of Saddam Hussein?*

✔ *Is the U.S. putting too much pressure on Israel—or not enough—to advance the Arab-Israeli peace process?*

BACKGROUND

The end of the cold war coupled with Iraqi President Saddam Hussein's invasion of Kuwait on Aug. 2, 1990, and its aftermath profoundly altered the political, economic and social map of the Middle East. The Gulf war, the first major post-cold-war crisis, united the international community against Iraq. On Aug. 6, the United Nations Security Council enacted mandatory trade and financial sanctions against Iraq. On Aug. 8, Iraq formally annexed Kuwait, and President George Bush outlined U.S. policy objectives in the Gulf: securing an unconditional withdrawal of all Iraqi forces from Kuwait, restoring Kuwait's legitimate government, maintaining security and stability in the Persian Gulf region, and protecting U.S. citizens. To achieve these goals, Bush assembled a multinational coalition of over 350,000 troops from 26 countries, in addition to 560,000 U.S. troops.

The sanctions failed to persuade Saddam Hussein to withdraw from Kuwait, and on Nov. 29, the UN autho-

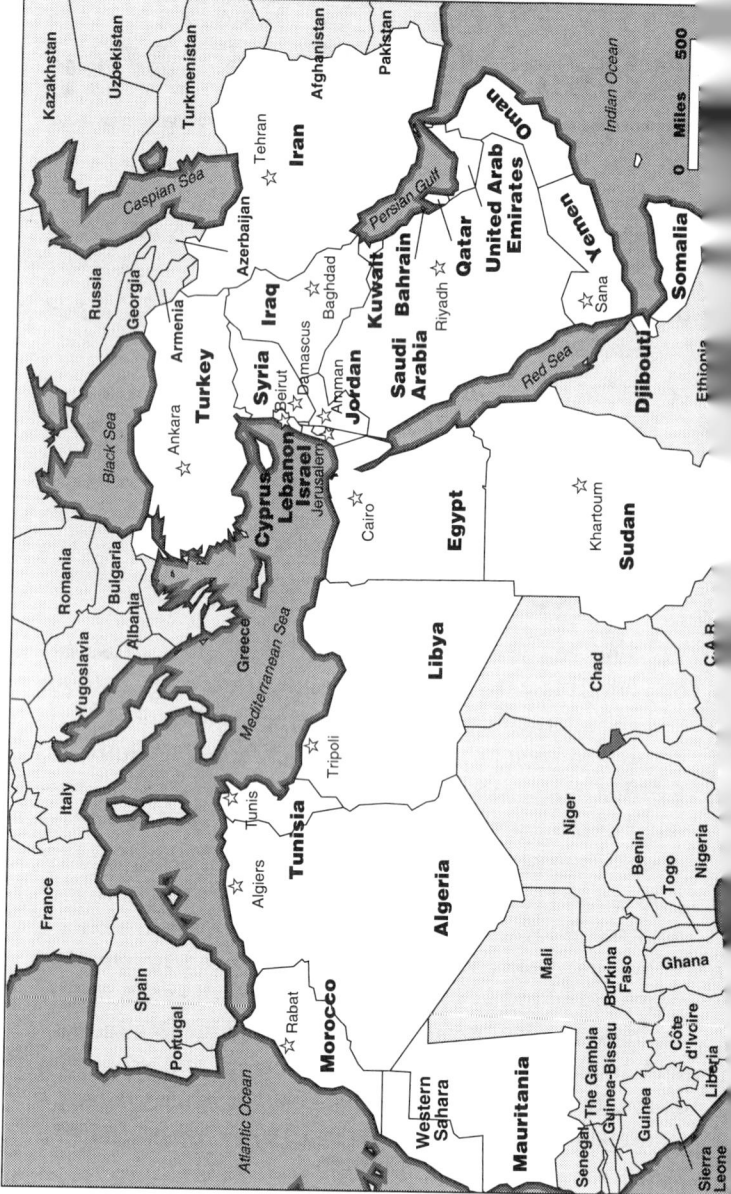

Robert Mansfield

Kazakhstan

Uzbekistan

Turkmenistan

Afghanistan

Pakistan

Iran

☆ Tehran

Caspian Sea

Russia

Georgia

Azerbaijan

Indian Ocean

Oman

United Arab Emirates

Yemen

Somalia

Armenia

Turkey

Iraq

Baghdad ☆

Kuwait

Bahrain

Qatar

☆ Ankara

Black Sea

Syria

Damascus

Riyadh ☆

Saudi Arabia

Sana ☆

Djibouti

Beirut

Jordan

Amman

Ethiopia

Lebanon

Israel

Persian Gulf

Red Sea

Jerusalem

Cyprus

☆ Cairo

Egypt

Khartoum ☆

Sudan

Romania

Bulgaria

Albania

Yugoslavia

Greece

Mediterranean Sea

Libya

Chad

C.A.R.

Italy

☆ Tripoli

Niger

France

Tunis ☆

Tunisia

Benin

Togo

Nigeria

Algiers ☆

Algeria

Ghana

Spain

Mali

Burkina Faso

Côte d'Ivoire

Portugal

☆ Rabat

Morocco

Atlantic Ocean

Western Sahara

Mauritania

Senegal

The Gambia

Guinea-Bissau

Guinea

Sierra Leone

Liberia

0   Miles   500

rized allied troops to use "all necessary means" to eject Iraq after Jan. 15, 1991. Diplomatic efforts to end the crisis also failed, and on Jan. 16 the allies began a six-week aerial bombardment of Iraq. On Feb. 23, after 38 days of continuous air strikes, the allies opened a ground offensive. After 100 hours of ground combat, the Iraqis were driven out of Kuwait and the U.S. declared victory. The U.S. suffered 148 fatalities; 38 deaths were the result of "friendly fire."

Saddam Hussein retained power, but the country was decimated. A UN team that visited Iraq in March 1991 found that aerial attacks had "wrought near apocalyptic results upon the infrastructure....Iraq has...been relegated to a preindustrial age." Food and medical supplies were seriously depleted and severe damage was sustained in three critical areas: electric power, telecommunications and the oil industry.

With U.S. encouragement, Shiite groups in southern Iraq (about 60% of the population) rebelled against Saddam Hussein but were crushed by his Republican Guards. Although American troops provided some protection to the Shiites, the U.S. did not support their rebellion. By mid-March, the Iraqi government had regained control of southern Iraq. In the north, Kurdish groups claimed control of most of Kurdistan. In early April, the Republican Guards attacked to reclaim the north, sending thousands of Kurds fleeing to Iran and Turkey. Many died on the way. On April 5 the UN Security Council passed Resolution 688, approving the establishment of "safe havens" protected by allied forces in northern Iraq. The Kurds were encouraged to return there.

On April 6, Iraq finally backed down and accepted UN Resolution 687 of April 3, which called for a continued arms embargo for an indefinite period; UN-supervised destruction of all Iraqi chemical and biological weapons, long-range ballistic missiles and nuclear arms production and storage sites; compensation to Kuwait and other countries for damages; the establishment of a demilitarized zone on the Kuwaiti border to be patrolled by UN peacekeepers; and UN demarcation of the border. On Aug. 15, 1991, the UN authorized Iraq to sell $1.6 billion worth of oil: 65% to pay for food and medicine, the remainder for reparations and UN peacekeeping expenses.

In the U.S., opponents of the war argued that it could have been avoided if only the U.S. had made it clear to Saddam Hussein that it was prepared to use military force against him. Eight days before the invasion, U.S. Ambassador to Iraq April Glaspie may have given Saddam Hussein the impression that the U.S. had no commitment to defend Kuwait. Opponents also criticized the Administration for helping to build up Iraq's war machine between 1983 and 1990 by allegedly authorizing the sale of billions of dollars worth of militarily useful technology and supplying U.S.-guaranteed loans for the purchase of grain, which Iraq reportedly used to buy weapons.

ARAB-ISRAELI PEACE TALKS

For decades, successive U.S. administrations have tried to broker a peace settlement in the Middle East. The end of the cold war and the Gulf war laid the groundwork for a new attempt at peacemaking that led to the convening of a Middle East peace conference in Oct. 1991. The talks were made possible by the ascendance of moderate states like Egypt and Saudi Arabia over radicals like Iraq and Syria, the decline of the pan-Arabist movement, the rise of new Palestinian leadership in the occupied territories, and Syrian President Hafez al-Assad's decision to seek reconciliation with the U.S. after he lost Soviet sponsorship. In exchange for his cooperation, the allies permitted Assad to install a pro-Syrian government in Lebanon, which had been torn by civil war since 1975. With the help of Syrian forces, the new Lebanese president, Elias Hrawi, regained control of Beirut and much of the countryside, enabling Lebanon to participate in the peace process.

Soon after the cease-fire in the Gulf, President Bush announced to a joint session of Congress on March 6,

Ed Gamble. Reprinted with special permission.
King Features Syndicate

1991, that the key challenge for U.S. policy in the Middle East was to find a solution to the Arab-Israeli conflict based on Israel's trading land that it has occupied since the 1967 war on the West Bank, the Gaza Strip and the Golan Heights for peace and Arab recognition. Between March and Oct. Secretary of State James A. Baker 3d made eight trips to the region to talk with Israeli, Egyptian, Syrian, Jordanian, Saudi Arabian and Palestinian leaders. Baker's shuttle diplomacy paid off when the peace talks opened in Madrid on Oct. 30. Delegations from Israel, Lebanon, Egypt and Jordan attended. Palestinian leaders living in the occupied territories participated in association with the Jordanian team.

Despite deep differences, the parties met face to face, which marked a turning point in the stalemated Arab-Israeli conflict. No substantive agreements have been reached and the talks have largely focused on procedural issues. The most recent round of direct, bilateral talks took place in April in Washington. Multilateral discussions, which complement the bilateral talks, opened in Moscow on Jan. 28–29 with delegates from Israel, 10 Arab nations, the European Community and several other countries to discuss regional problems such as water resources, refugees and arms control. The talks are on hold until after the Israeli election of June 23, which pits Labor party leader Yitzhak Rabin against Prime Minister Yitzhak Shamir, head of the hard-line Likud bloc.

U.S. efforts to extract Israeli concessions to move the peace talks forward have strained U.S.-Israeli relations. In early 1991 Israel sought U.S. loan guarantees to help absorb Soviet Jewish émigrés. It made the request for $10 billion formal on Sept. 6, 1991. Earlier the same day the President urged the U.S. Congress to defer consideration of the loan guarantees until Jan. to avoid a dispute with Israel that could abort the convening of a peace conference. Tensions between the two friends temporarily eased in Dec. 1991 when the UN General Assembly repealed the contentious 1975 UN resolution equating Zionism with racism. In Feb. Secretary of State Baker for the first time publicly stated that the $10 billion in loan guarantees were contingent on Israel's freezing all settlement activities in the occupied territories. Israel responded that it would accept no restrictions on its settlements and would not "beg or crawl" to obtain the guarantees. The Administration has not ruled out the possibility of an eventual compromise.

THE AFTERMATH OF THE GULF WAR

Operation Desert Storm achieved its strategic and military goals. Nonetheless, critics blame the Bush Administration for "winning the war but losing the peace" because Saddam Hussein is still in power, Iraqi compliance with UN resolutions is minimal, political reform in Kuwait and Saudi Arabia is virtually nonexistent, regional income disparities persist and threaten long-term stability, arms sales to the Middle East are increasing, and new security structures have not been implemented.

■ **GULF SECURITY:** Although Saddam Hussein's overthrow was not a specific war objective, critics claim the Bush Administration halted the war prematurely. Despite heavy losses, Iraq remains a significant military power with larger and better-equipped armed forces than most nations in the region. Iraq has not fully complied with UN Resolution 687, it has interfered with UN inspection and dismantling of its arms supplies, and it has also violated UN resolutions calling for the protection of minorities by shelling and shooting thousands of Kurdish civilians in their "safe havens."

On March 6, 1991, officials from the six Gulf Cooperation Council (GCC) states—Bahrain, Kuwait, Oman, Qatar, Saudi Arabia and United Arab Emirates—met with Egypt and Syria in Damascus, Syria's capital, and issued a declaration calling for the creation of a combined military force (including the U.S.) to deal with future aggression in the region. But differences between the parties have prevented the plan's implementation.

■ **ARMS PROLIFERATION:** The Middle East, the site of many of the world's most volatile conflicts, has a chronic arms race. "Middle East countries exceed any other part of the Third World (and some of the industrial world) in the size of their armed forces and the quantity and quality of their armament," according to a U.S. official. A number have chemical and biological weapons (and probably, in the case of Israel, nuclear weapons) and the missiles to deliver them.

Regional arms control efforts have not been successful. Arms suppliers have been reluctant to limit their lucrative sales to the Middle East. In his March1991 address to Congress, President Bush declared that "It would be tragic if the nations of the Middle East and the Persian Gulf were now, in the wake of war, to embark on a new arms race," and he proposed a Middle East arms control initiative. Since that speech, the U.S. has transferred arms worth roughly $8.5 billion to the region, according to the Arms Control Association.

■ **ISLAMIC REVIVAL:** The influence of Islam has been growing. The Iranian revolution of 1979, led by Ayatollah

Ruhollah Khomeini, inspired fears in the West of an Islamic resurgence that would threaten the stability of friendly Middle Eastern governments and access to vital interests in the region. An Iranian-style revolution has not been duplicated, although Islamic parties have made gains in Egypt, Jordan, Kuwait, Algeria and Turkey. In Algeria, for example, the Front for Islamic Salvation (FIS), whose goal is to create an Islamic state based on the Iranian model, won a landslide victory in democratic elections in Dec. 1991. The Islamic victory alarmed Western governments, neighboring Middle Eastern nations and Algeria's regime, which cut short the democratic process and jailed over 500 FIS leaders in Jan. 1992.

Are Islamic parties and governments incompatible with democracy and U.S. interests in the region? Prof. Lisa Anderson of Columbia University's Middle East Institute, among others, argues that the threat of Islamic fundamentalism has been overestimated: "Most supporters of the Islamist movements are not hostile to the West but envious; they blame their own governments for failing to provide the well-being they know that Westerners take for granted….Whoever takes power in the Islamic world will face intractable economic problems."

ADMINISTRATION POLICY

■ **ARAB-ISRAELI PEACE PROCESS:** The Bush Administration maintains that the process launched in Madrid is the best means to achieve a comprehensive, lasting peace in the Middle East. The final agreement must include, according to the Administration, an exchange of land for peace; security and recognition for Israel; and acceptance of the legitimate political rights of the Palestinians. Secretary Baker has stated his intention to continue acting as a catalyst and impartial mediator. The presidential election campaign, however, has diverted the Administration's attention from foreign policy.

The Administration has attempted to downplay the tensions between Bush and Shamir over the question of

loan guarantees by emphasizing the close relationship between the two nations over more than 40 years. "Our
commitment to Israel's well-being and its security, including its qualitative military edge over any likely com-
bination of aggressors, remains unshakeable," Secretary
Baker declared. "As democracies, the U.S. and Israel
share similar values and common traditions that have
provided a strong foundation for cooperation."

■ **GULF SECURITY:** The Administration considers stability
in the Gulf region vital to the U.S. national interest and
global economic security. In a speech to the Foreign
Policy Association, Assistant Secretary of State for Near
East and South Asian Affairs Edward P. Djerejian
stressed "the need for individual self-defense, and for collective defense planning and action among the six GCC
states, with the goal of strengthening their ability to defend themselves from external aggression." The U.S. has
assured its Gulf allies of its commitment to meet their defense needs by weapons sales and bilateral security arrangements. At the same time, the Administration's arms
control initiative is aimed at controlling transfers of conventional weapons and weapons of mass destruction.

Iraq remains the most immediate threat to Gulf security, in Washington's view. The Administration is determined to block Saddam Hussein's military ambitions by
maintaining a tough stance vis-à-vis Iraq. At the same
time, the U.S. supports the international community's
commitment to programs of humanitarian assistance to
the Iraqi people.

The U.S. must decide when to reestablish relations
with Iran. The Bush Administration's long-term condi-
tion—release of the hostages in Lebanon—has now been
met.

POLICY CHOICES

1. SECURITY:
A. Be prepared to intervene unilaterally to protect U.S.

strategic and economic interests in the Middle East.

OR

B. Rely on the UN and regional powers to maintain the peace in the region.

2. ISRAEL:

A. Strengthen relations and avoid interfering in internal affairs, including tying loans to a settlement freeze.

OR

B. Increase pressure on Israel to make concessions to advance the Arab-Israeli peace process.

3. ARMS EXPORTS:

A. Continue selling arms to the Middle East. If the U.S. holds back, others will satisfy customer demands.

OR

B. Promote the banning of weapons of mass destruction in the Middle East and control shipments of conventional arms to that region.

SELECT BIBLIOGRAPHY

Djerejian, Edward P., "The Middle East: US Interests and Challenges Ahead." *US Department of State Dispatch,* March 23, 1992, pp. 218–20. Statement before the House Committee on Foreign Affairs outlining U.S. policies on current issues in the Middle East.

"The Middle East after Desert Storm: As the Dust Settles." *Great Decisions 1992,* pp. 15–24. New York, Foreign Policy Association, 1992. Examines the prospects for Mideast peace after the Gulf war.

Muslih, Muhammad, and Norton, Augustus Richard, "Political Tides in the Middle East." *Headline Series* No. 296. New York, Foreign Policy Association, Summer 1991. Why the Gulf war marked a turning point in the politics of the Middle East.

Stein, Kenneth W., and Lewis, Samuel W., et al., *Making Peace Among Arabs and Israelis: Lessons from Fifty Years of Negotiating Experience.* Washington D.C., U.S. Institute of Peace, Oct. 1991. Outlines necessary elements for an Arab-Israeli peace and discusses problems encountered during the peace process.

8

United Nations and Peacekeeping

✔ *Should the U.S. pay its past and current UN dues?*

✔ *Has the UN undertaken too many peacekeeping missions?*

✔ *Would you support a change in the composition of the Security Council?*

BASIC FACTS

- UN Charter signed in San Francisco in 1945; 51 original member-states; now 175.

- Principal organs: the General Assembly, in which each state has one vote; the Security Council, comprising five permanent members with veto power (Britain, China, France, Russia and the U.S.), and 10 rotating members, elected to two-year terms; 54-member Economic and Social Council; International Court of Justice (World Court); Secretariat, based in New York City.

- Secretary-general: Boutros Ghali of Egypt, elected in 1991 to a five-year term.

- UN specialized agencies include the World Bank, the World Health Organization (WHO), the Food and Agriculture Organization (FAO), the International Labor Organization (ILO).

- UN agencies funded by voluntary contributions include the UN Development Program (UNDP), the UN Environment Program (UNEP) and the UN Children's Fund (Unicef).

- UN regular budget in 1992: $1.2 billion; U.S. share (25%)—$299 million.

- U.S. arrears to UN system at end of 1991—$256 million; U.S. arrears to UN peacekeeping—$112 million.

- Peacekeeping: 12 current operations; 1991 budget—$715 million; 1992 projected budget, $2.7 billion.

BACKGROUND

The UN's many goals include maintaining international peace and security, cooperating to solve economic, social, cultural and humanitarian problems, and safeguarding human rights and basic freedoms. But for most of its existence the UN membership has been polarized between Western democracies, Communist countries and the developing nations (Third World), including the so-called nonaligned. In 1985, to protest what it perceived as the world body's anti-U.S. bias and mismanagement, the U.S. Congress passed the Kassebaum amendment, limiting the U.S. contribution to the UN regular operating budget to 20% unless the UN adopted a system of weighted voting on budgetary matters.

In the late 1980s, in a marked shift in the U.S.S.R.'s position, Soviet President Mikhail S. Gorbachev called for more UN involvement in solving world problems and moved to pay his country's back dues. In the U.S., first President Ronald Reagan and then President George Bush asked Congress to resume paying UN dues in full and to catch up on arrears. The cold war was ending.

The former enemies' willingness to work together paved the way for a series of successes that bolstered the UN's international standing:

- in 1988, the Soviet agreement to withdraw from Afghanistan and the end of the Iran-Iraq War;
- in 1989, the start of the removal of Cuban troops from Angola;

Robert Mansfield

UNTAC Cambodia

UNIKOM Iraq/Kuwait

UNMOGIP India/Pakistan

UNOSOM Somalia

UNDOF Syria

UNIFIL Lebanon

UNPROFOR Yugoslavia

UNTSO Israel, Lebanon, Jordan, Syria and Egypt

UNFICYP Cypress

MINURSO West Sahara

UNIVEM II West Sahara

ONUSAL El Salvador

Where UN Forces Keep the Peace

- in 1990, the independence of Namibia and the election of a democratic government in Nicaragua;
- in 1991, the end of Angola's civil war, the Iraqi withdrawal from Kuwait, the release of Western hostages in Lebanon, the signing of a peace accord in Cambodia and the truce in El Salvador.

Demands for UN intervention in new situations are rapidly rising, from election-monitoring to safeguarding human rights. Industrialized nations tend to support UN action on behalf of human rights, while developing nations tend to oppose it. Protecting human rights was among the topics discussed at the Jan. 1992 Security Council summit of heads of state. Russian Federation President Boris N. Yeltsin said that human rights "are not an internal matter of states, but rather obligations under the UN Charter"; China strongly opposed intervention in countries' internal affairs "using human rights as an excuse."

■ **BUDGET:** The UN's regular budget and the budgets of most specialized agencies come from dues levied on member-states based on their capacity to pay. The U.S., with the largest economy, is assessed the maximum rate, or 25%, of the UN regular budget. About 80 members pay the minimum rate, or 0.01%.

Budget shortfalls have consistently plagued the UN. At the end of 1991, members owed the UN's regular budget arrearages totaling $439 million. The U.S. was the biggest debtor ($256 million), followed by Russia ($46 million), South Africa ($45 million), Brazil ($17.8 million) and Ukraine ($5.7 million).

The Kassebaum amendment has been revised, and the U.S. began paying its back dues in FY1991. For FY1992 Congress approved the Bush Administration's request for $750 million to pay full dues to the UN and its organizations, plus $371 million to pay off arrearages over the next four years. The Administration also requested about $250 million for voluntary contributions to UN programs in FY1992, the bulk of it for the UNDP and Unicef. In recent years, Congress has consistently authorized more than the Administration has requested for such agencies.

■ **PEACEKEEPING:** UN peacekeepers, or "blue helmets," have traditionally been dispatched to supervise truces, man buffer zones and patrol borders. Their presence requires the consent of the warring parties and they are not allowed to take sides in conflicts.Since the first peacekeepers were sent to Palestine in 1948, 25 peacekeeping forces have been established, 12 between Jan. 1988 and April 1992 alone. In 1988, the UN was awarded the Nobel Peace Prize for its peacekeeping activities.

Peacekeepers' roles and responsibilities have greatly expanded. Recent missions have included ensuring free elections (Namibia, Nicaragua and Haiti), disarming combatants (Nicaragua) and responding to humanitarian emergencies (Iraq, Bangladesh and the Horn of Africa). Four operations were launched in 1991: along the Iraq-Kuwaiti border, in El Salvador, Angola and Western Sahara. Three more got under way in 1992, in Cambodia, Yugoslavia and Somalia. The Iraq-Kuwaiti operation costs $80 million and involves 540 troops. The Cambodian mission, the largest ever undertaken by the UN, which includes administering the country together with the Supreme National Council, helping organize elections in 1993, overseeing the repatriation of 350,000 refugees and disarming of four warring groups, involves 22,000 personnel at an estimated cost $1.9 billion. (See Chapter 9.) The Yugoslav operation has a force of 15,100; the estimated cost is more than $600 million.

Peacekeeping costs for the most part are assessed, with the UN Security Council's five permanent members carrying most of the burden because of their special responsibility for preserving international security. (Humanitarian operations, on the other hand, are funded by voluntary contributions.) The U.S. is automatically responsible for 30.4% of the cost of each peacekeeping operation. At the start of 1992 members collectively owed $377 million in peacekeeping fees. The U.S. was one of the two biggest delinquents, owing $112 million; Russia owed $127 million.

In a time of recession, Congress is balking at paying peacekeeping costs, which are expected to triple this year. Congress initially appropriated $207 million for peacekeeping in 1992; the Bush Administration then asked for an additional $350 million to fund the Yugoslavia and Cambodia operations. Secretary of State James A. Baker 3d got a frosty reception when he went before Congress in March 1992 to defend the request. When Congress voted in April, it only appropriated an additional $270 million, $80 million less than Bush wanted.

Critics question the fairness of the U.S. paying 30% of the cost. They note that Germany and Japan pay 6.9% and 12.5%, respectively. Some critics would have regional organizations and major powers close to the nations in conflict bear more of the cost., e.g., Japan in the case of Cambodia, the European Community in the case of Yugoslavia. (Japan has already pledged to pay half the cost of the Cambodian operation.) Some object to peacekeeping as another form of unpopular foreign aid. Peacekeeping is funded by the State Department but is not part of foreign aid. Sen. Paul Simon (D-Ill.) has proposed that the cost of peacekeeping be shifted to the Defense Department. Former U.S. Secretary of State and UN special envoy Cyrus R. Vance has endorsed Simon's legislation, saying that crucial international peacekeeping efforts require "a fresh approach" by the U.S.

Pressure is rising to establish a permanent fund for peacekeeping. The General Assembly has expressed support for a $50 million reserve fund to help launch new peacekeeping operations. A 1992 study by the Washington-based Henry L. Stimson Center recommends making peacemaking an integral part of the annual UN budget. In Jan., Security Council heads of state asked the secretary-general to place new emphasis on "preventive diplomacy": solving disputes before they erupt into conflicts that then require expensive peacekeeping operations.

■ **USE OF FORCE:** The Security Council is the UN body responsible for maintaining peace and settling disputes.

Articles 43–47 of the Charter call on members to make available "in accordance with a special agreement or agreements, armed forces, assistance and facilities" to maintain international peace. They also provide for a Military Staff Committee that is to advise the Security Council on military action. But no such forces were ever put at the Security Council's disposal, nor did the Military Staff Committee ever function in the cold-war environment. On only one occasion, when North Korea invaded South Korea in 1950, did the UN undertake military action. (The Soviet Union was temporarily boycotting the Security Council.) In the case of the Iraqi invasion of Kuwait, although the Security Council backed the use of military force, the coalition troops did not fly the UN banner.

The UN's dependence on voluntary manpower to take military action has raised questions regarding possible manipulation of the world body by the contributing nations, the quality and leadership of the UN forces, and the troops' loyalty to their country vs. their loyalty to the UN. In the case of the war against Iraq, critics accused the UN of becoming an instrument of U.S. foreign policy.

Those who believe the UN should have military forces at its command say they would enhance the UN's credibility and authority. But some of the larger nations feel such a force might interfere with their own freedom of action, while smaller nations fear it might be used to discipline them. Among the unresolved questions are the cost, composition and command of a UN force. France in Jan. offered to provide the Security Council with troops for a rapid deployment force that could swing into action quickly in an emergency.

■ **SECURITY COUNCIL:** Debate is increasing over revising the composition and size of the Security Council. Both Japan and Germany, which have become major economic powers and important UN contributors, want permanent seats, as do some of the larger developing countries such as Brazil, Egypt, India and Nigeria. Italy has called for "weighted voting," whereby members' power in the council would be determined by population or financial contributions. Smaller nations have long favored revamping the council on the grounds that they are under-represented in the "big boys" club. The permanent members, who have the final say, have tended to oppose any changes that would affect their status. Another question is whether to revise the rules governing the veto power. (Decisions on substantive measures currently require nine votes to pass, including the votes of all five permanent members.) When the General Assembly discussed Security Council changes in 1991 for the first time in a number of years, there was strong support for change among both developed and developing nations.

ADMINISTRATION POLICY

The Bush Administration considers the UN a key tool for implementing the President's vision of a new world order that stresses international peace, the rule of law and a cooperative approach to security. "We seek a 'Pax Universalis' built upon shared responsibilities and aspirations," Bush told the UN General Assembly in Sept. 1991.

Although the Administration supports paying current UN assessments and arrears to the UN regular budget, it rejected a 1991 proposal by former Secretary General Pérez de Cuéllar to increase assessments, saying countries were having a hard enough time meeting present obligations and that better use needed to be made of existing funds.

The Administration is also leery of the rising costs of peacekeeping, although it considers them a "forward defense" and an investment in peace. Secretary Baker, under pressure from Congress, has ordered a review of this country's 30% budget assessment. The U.S. does not support changing the composition of the Security Council or the rules governing veto power, saying the council is just beginning to function as envisioned by the UN Charter. The U.S. is reluctant to create an enforcement arm for the UN because it might interfere with its own autonomy and freedom to carry out military action.

POLICY CHOICES

1. U.S. AND UN:
A. Put this country's full support behind the UN's political, economic and social activities at a time when international collaboration is showing the greatest promise.

OR

B. Confine support to UN social and humanitarian activities because it is too politicized, mismanaged and overextended to be the guarantor of international peace.

2. PEACEKEEPING:
A. Fully fund present and future UN peacekeeping operations.

OR

B. Reduce U.S. contribution to UN peacekeeping operations.

3. SECURITY COUNCIL:
A. Restructure Security Council because current composition does not reflect today's balance of power.

OR

B. Keep present structure. Change would diminish effectiveness of the Security Council, which is just now starting to operate as UN Charter envisioned.

SELECT BIBLIOGRAPHY

Daley, Tad, "Can the UN Stretch to Fit its Future?" *The Bulletin of the Atomic Scientists,* April 1992, pp. 38–42. Discussion of new roles for the UN and possible reforms.

Laurenti, Jeffrey, *The Common Defense: Peace and Security in a Changing World.* United Nations Association of the United States of America, 485 Fifth Ave., New York, N.Y. 10017, 1992. A survey of security issues facing the UN after the end of the cold war and the Persian Gulf crisis.

Norton, Augustus Richard, and Weiss, Thomas George, "UN Peacekeepers: Soldiers with a Difference." *Headline Series* No. 292. New York, Foreign Policy Association, 1990. Survey of history of peacekeeping and possible new roles in the future.

"The United Nations in a New Era." *US Department of State Dispatch,* Sept. 30, 1991, pp. 718–22. Includes President George Bush's address before the UN General Assembly, profile of the UN and fact sheet on peacekeeping operations.

"United Nations: New Life for an Aging Institution?" *Great Decisions 1990,* pp. 59–68. New York, Foreign Policy Association, 1990. Overview of UN's history, global role and U.S. policy.

9

Vietnam and Cambodia

✔ *Should the U.S. establish diplomatic relations with Vietnam?*

✔ *What role should the U.S. play in Cambodia?*

BACKGROUND

For most Americans, Vietnam and Cambodia conjure up images of the bitter war to prevent Communists from taking power in Indochina that the U.S. helped fight from the 1960s to the mid-1970s. U.S. relations with the region, minimal since the end of that war, have remained focused on two continuing issues: the status of Americans still listed as prisoners of war or missing in action (POW/MIAs) and the fate of Indochinese refugees fleeing their homeland.

Indochina, the region comprising Vietnam, Cambodia and Laos, was occupied by France for almost a century. The Vietnamese struggle for independence from France (1946–54), led by the Communist Ho Chi Minh, was the first of three major wars to embroil the region after World War II. In 1953, France granted independence to Cambodia and Laos. In 1954 it granted Vietnam full independence in association with France. The French forces withdrew from Vietnam after their defeat by the Vietminh at Dien Bien Phu, leaving the north of the country under the control of Ho Chi Minh. Under the terms of the armistice concluded at an international conference in Geneva, Switzerland, in 1954, Vietnam was to be temporarily divided into a Communist-administered

North, with its capital in Hanoi, and a non-Communist administered South until internationally supervised elections, which were scheduled for 1956. The government of South Vietnam, based in Saigon, rejected this plan and as a result the elections were never held and the country remained divided.

In the second war (1960–75), South Vietnam, with U.S. backing, fought and ultimately lost power to a Communist insurgency supported by North Vietnam, the Soviet Union and China. Over 55,000 American servicemen died in Vietnam. A final peace agreement was signed in Jan. 1973 and called for a cease-fire, a withdrawal of U.S. troops, the release of POWs and U.S. aid for the postwar reconstruction of North Vietnam. The North continued to infiltrate the South, and in April 1975 Saigon fell to the North Vietnamese forces. The two halves of the country were reunited.

The Vietnam War, the first that the U.S. "lost," bitterly divided Americans and fostered distrust of their government. It marked a turning point in U.S. foreign policy and the end of the post-World War II bipartisan consensus between the executive and legislative branches. Since then Congress has taken a more assertive role in foreign policy. The war led to a loss of U.S. prestige in the world and gave rise to the term "Vietnam syndrome," meaning a new reluctance to get involved abroad. The debate over who lost Vietnam will undoubtedly continue, but many would agree with journalist Stanley Karnow, who observed it was a "war nobody won."

■ **CAMBODIA INVADED:** Although both Vietnam and Cambodia were under Communist control, old ethnic antagonisms persisted. Vietnam invaded Cambodia in Dec. 1978, inaugurating a third Indochina war. Vietnam drove out the Khmer Rouge, the fanatical Khmer (Cambodian) nationalists led by the notorious Pol Pot and supported by China, who had imposed a reign of terror on Cambodia, killing upward of a million people. (Cambodia's present population is about 7 million.) The Khmer Rouge re-

Indochina

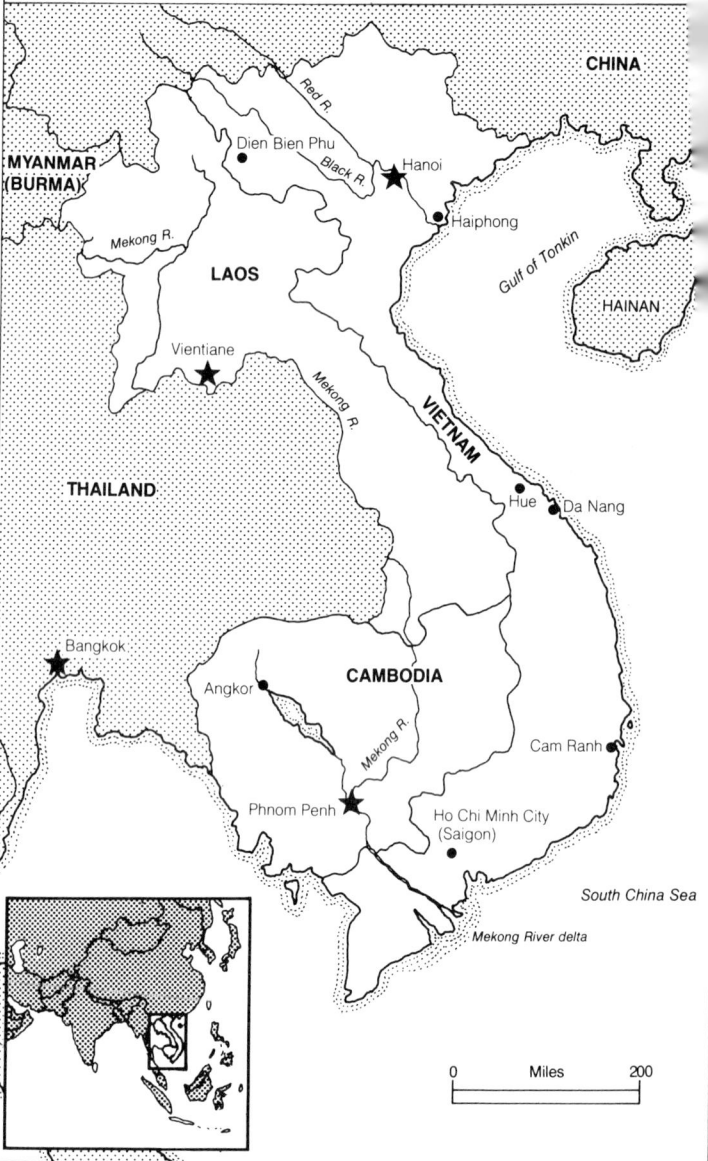

CHINA

MYANMAR
(BURMA)

Red R.

Dien Bien Phu

Black R.

Hanoi

Haiphong

Mekong R.

Gulf of Tonkin

LAOS

HAINAN

Vientiane

Mekong R.

VIETNAM

THAILAND

Hue

Da Nang

Bangkok

Angkor

CAMBODIA

Mekong R.

Cam Ranh

Phnom Penh

Ho Chi Minh City
(Saigon)

South China Sea

Mekong River delta

0   Miles   200

Robert Mansfield

treated to sanctuaries near the border with Thailand. Along with two non-Communist groups, the most prominent of which was headed by former head of state Prince Norodom Sihanouk (1941–70), they harassed the Vietnamese-installed government led by Hun Sen. Vietnamese troops occupied Cambodia for a decade before withdrawing in Sept. 1989. Since then, outside powers have tried to mediate a solution.

Resolution of the civil war was made possible by the ending of the cold war and the warming of relations between the U.S. and the Soviet Union. In Oct. 1991, the five permanent members of the United Nations Security Council (Britain, China, France, the Soviet Union and the U.S.) met in Paris and brokered a peace treaty aimed at ending the conflict in Cambodia. The three opposition groups, led by Prince Sihanouk, former Prime Minister Son Sann and the Khmer Rouge, and the Hun Sen government accepted the UN proposal. The new accords provided for a cease-fire and the demobilization of 70% of existing forces, the return of approximately 350,000 Cambodians from refugee camps, and the administration of the country by the UN until free elections can be held in 1993. Prince Sihanouk made a triumphant return to Cambodia in Nov. and was named president. However, the Khmer Rouge have been guaranteed a role in the government, which frightens many.

CURRENT STATUS

■ **VIETNAM** is one of the world's poorest countries, with an annual per capita income of $195. This is largely due to a U.S. trade embargo, imposed in 1975, which has prevented the country from receiving aid from the World Bank and the International Monetary Fund. Aid from the Soviet Union, once substantial, has now been cut off. Hanoi introduced a dramatic economic liberalization program in 1986 that has led to foreign investment, mainly in the south, and has resulted in a more realistic exchange rate. In Saigon (officially Ho Chi Minh City), capitalism rather than communism is the motivating force. However, serious problems such as a lack of infrastructure, the uncertain political situation, continuing inflation and corruption have kept many investors away.

The disintegration of the Soviet Union led to rapprochement between Vietnam and China, its traditional enemy. It also hardened the determination of Vietnamese leaders not to relax their control or institute political reforms. Repression and poor economic conditions have caused thousands of Vietnamese to emigrate, many in rickety boats, to nearby countries. This outflow has slowed since Hong Kong began forcibly sending refugees back home. The U.S. opposed this forced repatriation, but would not agree to accept the refugees for resettlement.

Vietnam is eager to end its international isolation, and when it does so, conditions for the country's 67.6 million people are bound to improve. The next key step is for a resumption of U.S. ties.

■ **CAMBODIA:** As a result of the Oct. 1991 agreements, the UN has "transitional authority" in Cambodia. The mandate of the UN Transitional Authority in Cambodia (Untac) is to monitor the cease-fire, the demobilization of more than 200,000 troops of the former warring factions and arrangements for placing them in temporary camps, to share governing powers with the Supreme National Council and to help organize the elections.

The budget for this undertaking, the most ambitious ever attempted by the UN, is $1.9 billion and will involve 16,000 soldiers and 6,000 civilian administrators. Although the project is vital for the future of Cambodia, its degree of success will also affect the extent of future UN interventions in other parts of the world.

In April 1992, the leaders of Cambodia's four factions signed two international charters committing them to respect human rights. Although only Prince Sihanouk, as head of the coalition, needed to sign the covenants, the UN asked all four to commit themselves because of the appalling human-rights record of the Khmer Rouge.

Many still consider the Khmer Rouge to be the greatest long-term threat to peace in Cambodia.

The UN effort has hit a few snags. Only a small number of the promised 16,000 troops have arrived in Cambodia, delaying the demobilization of the Cambodian soldiers. Also, questions of jurisdiction of various UN agencies have arisen. For example, the demobilized soldiers will not be considered refugees, and it is not clear who will cover the cost of the temporary camps and eventual resettlement. Funding in general is proving to be a problem. Washington's share is 30.4% of the total, or $577 million for an 18-month period. However, the U.S. Congress has pledged only $270 million for *all* UN peacekeeping, with $200 million of that earmarked for the Cambodia operation.

ADMINISTRATION POLICY

The Bush Administration, following the policy of its predecessor, set three conditions for normalization of relations with Hanoi: a Vietnamese troop withdrawal from Cambodia, a political settlement there, and assistance in accounting for about 2,300 U.S. POWs and MIAs from the Vietnam War. At the UN, the U.S. tolerated the Khmer Rouge representing Cambodia on the grounds that recognizing the Hun Sen government, which was imposed by force, would set a bad precedent. In Cambodia, the U.S. has supported a leading role for Prince Sihanouk, whom it regards as the only one who can unify the country and achieve international legitimacy.

After the withdrawal of Vietnamese troops and the conclusion of a Cambodian peace accord, the U.S. took a small step toward normalizing relations with Hanoi. It lifted a ban on travel to Vietnam by U.S.-organized groups. However, as public pressure built in early 1992 for a full accounting of the POWs, spurred by alleged sightings of live Americans in Vietnam, Washington put the normalization process on hold. The Vietnamese government denies that it holds any POWs. Since 1985 it has permitted U.S. teams to search sites in Vietnam. In April 1991 Vietnam permitted the U.S. to open an MIA office in Hanoi. While the U.S. government does not rule out the possibility that Vietnam and Laos still hold prisoners, it has not yet received what it regards as credible evidence. Some individuals and organizations, nevertheless, believe that the U.S. government has covered up such evidence.

The same month that it was authorized to open the MIA office, the U.S. indicated that after the UN transitional administration was established in Cambodia and there was a final resolution of the MIA issue, it would gradually remove its trade embargo on Vietnam and exchange diplomatic missions.

The U.S. sent its first diplomatic representative in 16 years to Cambodia in Nov. 1991. In Jan. 1992 President Bush announced the lifting of a 16-year-old U.S. trade embargo and announced the U.S. would support World Bank projects there. The main U.S. aim is to prevent the Khmer Rouge from returning to power and to assure free and fair elections in Cambodia. After that, it will restore full diplomatic relations.

POLICY CHOICES

1. VIETNAM:
A. Recognize Vietnam. It has fulfilled all the conditions set by the U.S. for normalization. Continuation of the U.S. trade embargo unfairly punishes Vietnamese, keeps U.S. business away.

OR

B. Continue to withhold recognition until Vietnam releases conclusive information on POW/MIAs and adopts political reforms, including respect for human rights.

2. CAMBODIA:
A. Pay our share of UN peacekeeping expenses. It is a small price to pay for peace in the region.

OR

B. Let regional powers, with a more direct stake in Cambodia's future, pay the lion's share of the UN peace-keeping operation.

SELECT BIBLIOGRAPHY

Clark, Dick, *The Challenge of Indochina: An Examination of the U.S. Role.* Aspen, Colo., Institute for Humanistic Studies, 1991.

"Comprehensive Political Settlement for Cambodia Signed in Paris." *Foreign Policy Bulletin,* Nov.–Dec. 1991, pp. 30–34. Statement by Secretary of State James A. Baker 3d at Paris Conference on Cambodia, Oct. 23, 1991, statement by assistant secretary of state on Cambodia settlement, and text of final act.

Shenon, Philip, "Reaching for the Good Life in Vietnam." *The New York Times Magazine,* Jan. 5, 1992, pp.16 +. The chief of the *Times'* Bangkok bureau writes that although the North won the war, the South is winning the peace. Photographs by Andrew Holbrooke.

"Vietnam, Cambodia and the U.S.: Return Engagement?" *Great Decisions 1990,* pp. 37–47. New York, Foreign Policy Association, 1990. Impartial background and analysis of developments in Indochina and U.S. policy.

10

China and the U.S.

✔ *Should the U.S. continue to grant China special trade status?*

✔ *Should respect for human rights be a precondition for improved relations?*

BASIC FACTS

The People's Republic of China

- Population: 1.2 billion

- Gross national product (GNP): $356 billion

- U.S.-China trade (1991): $25.3 billion

- U.S. trade deficit with China: $12.7 billion

- China's exports to U.S. as percentage of total exports: 26%

BACKGROUND

America's refusal to recognize the People's Republic of China (PRC), founded on Oct. 1, 1949, as the legitimate government of China, smoldering antipathy from the Korean War (1950–53), and a formal U.S. alliance with the Nationalist government in Taiwan contributed to 30 years of frosty Sino-American relations.

The PRC's diplomatic isolation ended when it received enough votes to take the Chinese seat at the United Nations in 1971. President Richard M. Nixon's trip to Beijing in 1972 began a warming trend that culminated in China receiving U.S. diplomatic recognition on Jan. 1, 1979. China's agreement to normalize relations was contingent on the U.S. breaking formal diplomatic ties and terminating its mutual defense treaty with Taiwan and withdrawing its troops.

As a result of better relations, President Jimmy Carter and Vice Premier Deng Xiaoping met in early 1979 to discuss trade relations. In Oct., Carter sent a Sino-American trade agreement to Congress and signed a proclamation waiving the Jackson-Vanik amendment to the Trade Act of 1974, which prohibits granting most-favored-nation (MFN) status to Communist countries that restrict emigration. Congress approved MFN status for China in Jan. 1980, and a major bilateral trade pact was signed that Sept. MFN status is subject to annual review.

The army's violent crackdown on prodemocracy student protesters in Tiananmen Square, Beijing, on June 3-4, 1989, temporarily halted Sino-American cooperation. In the aftermath of what the Chinese government prefers to call the counterrevolutionary rebellion, hard-liners in the Communist hierarchy used police intimidation and court trials to suppress political opposition. On June 5, the Bush Administration suspended military sales and postponed high-level military exchanges. The U.S. also gave refuge to Fang Lizhi, a prominent Chinese dissident, in the U.S. embassy. On June 20, Washington imposed additional sanctions, which called for the postponement of loans by international financial institutions and suspension of visits by high-level U.S. officials to China.

At the same time, the Administration took the position that the isolation of the PRC, a nuclear power with vast economic potential, was counterproductive. Demonstrating his commitment to maintaining good Sino-American relations, the President in spite of the sanctions authorized his national security adviser, Brent Scowcroft, to make a secret trip to China in early July. President George Bush later explained that the trip was taken "to personally underscore the U.S. shock and concern" over Tiananmen Square and its aftermath. When Scowcroft returned to Beijing in Dec., his visit was announced only after his team had arrived in China.

THE MFN DEBATE

In mid-summer 1989, many legislators, critical of the Administration for not imposing stricter sanctions, attempted to tie MFN status to Chinese observance of human rights. After the fall of communism in 1989–90 in Eastern Europe, the MFN debate grew more intense. House majority leader Richard A. Gephardt (D-Mo.) noted, "At a time when America's bipartisan commitment to freedom is bearing fruit in Eastern Europe, the last thing [the President] should be doing is wavering in our commitment to freedom in China." Critics of the Administration claimed that the end of the cold war had diminished China's strategic importance to the U.S. Therefore, China's trade privileges should be curtailed until it changed its human-rights policy and released political prisoners. The Administration disagreed on the grounds that restrictions on Chinese imports would be counterproductive and that the U.S. was beholden to China for its support in the UN Security Council in opposing the Iraqi invasion of Kuwait. In Nov. 1990, the House voted to rescind MFN status for China, but the Senate took no action on the bill, ensuring the continuation of MFN through June 1991.

During a trip to China in May 1991, Under Secretary of State for Political Affairs Robert Kimmitt warned that a presidential waiver of requirements for MFN status was not guaranteed. Nevertheless, on May 15 President Bush announced his intention to renew China's MFN privileges. Bills designed to terminate or place conditions on China's MFN privileges ran into opposition not only from the Administration but from a formidable bloc of pro-Hong Kong groups, Sino-American business organizations, members of the academic community and some senators. On March 19, 1992, the Senate approved a bill placing conditions on China's MFN status; it fell seven votes short of overriding the presidential veto.

Mike Luckovich.
By permission of Mike Luckovich and Creators Syndicate.

HUMAN RIGHTS

Beijing's human-rights record, including the repression of Tibet and the treatment of dissenters, has long been a source of tension between China and the U.S. After Tiananmen the tensions escalated. In March 1990, the U.S. published its annual human-rights report on China. While previous reports had emphasized positive movement in China's human-rights policy, this one condemned Beijing for its persistent use of torture, the use of coercion in its family-planning program and other violations. President Bush's meeting in April with the Dalai Lama, the exiled spiritual leader of Tibet, was viewed as an expression of the Administration's impatience with Chinese intransigence on human rights.

The Administration favors "quiet diplomacy" to influence China's human-rights policies. It does not believe Beijing will respond to pressure such as suspension of trade privileges. It points to Beijing's concessions in the spring of 1990—including the release of almost 800 detainees and permission for Fang Lizhi to take up residence in the U.S.—as vindication for its approach.

Critics of Bush's China policy charge that human rights have not improved significantly since Tiananmen. Some prominent activists have been released but many lesser-known figures are still in prison or labor camps. According to Timothy A. Gelatt, professor of Chinese law at New York University, "The only positive actions the Chinese government has taken on human rights since Tiananmen have come in the face of key sanctions decisions."

The U.S. has successfully used selective tariffs to obtain economic concessions from China. A similar approach could be used to force changes in China's human-rights policy, suggests Holly Burkhalter, Washington director of Human Rights Watch: "Tariff penalties should be selectively imposed and incrementally increased until significant numbers of prisoners are released, basic religious freedoms respected and labor camps and prisons opened for international inspection."

OTHER ISSUES IN THE SINO-AMERICAN DIALOGUE

■ **TRADE DEFICIT:** In 1980, total Sino-American trade was valued at $4.8 billion. By 1990, China had become America's tenth-largest trading partner, with bilateral trade totaling $20 billion. During the late 1980s, as U.S. imports outstripped exports, the U.S. developed a trade deficit with China second only to its deficit with Japan. Many observers attribute the deficit to Chinese restrictive trade practices, devaluations in China's currency and foreign-exchange controls.

■ **U.S. INTELLECTUAL PROPERTY VIOLATIONS:** In 1989, China was placed on the U.S. "priority watch list" of countries accused of stealing intellectual property (patents and copyrights). It was removed that May after signing a memorandum of understanding with the U.S., but

Danziger. The Christian Science Monitor© 1991 TCSPS

was reinstated on the list in April 1991. In Jan. 1992, after U.S. Trade Representative Carla Hills threatened to impose tariffs on certain key Chinese exports, China signed another memorandum agreeing to bolster its patent, copyright and trade-secret laws, and the U.S. terminated the investigation of Chinese violations.

■ **PRISON-MADE EXPORTS:** Some Chinese exports are allegedly manufactured by prisoners detained for their roles in the prodemocracy movement. Although the allegations are difficult to confirm, evidence of widespread use of prison labor has been found in official Chinese documents. With the Administration's support, Congress in Nov. and Dec. 1991 enacted several bans on the importation of prison-made products.

■ **ARMS SUPPLIER TO THE THIRD WORLD:** Although China reportedly has increased military spending by 50% since 1989, causing concern to its neighbors and U.S. policymakers, in the 1980s Deng Xiaoping slashed China's military budget. To make up for the cuts in its budget, the army increased arms exports. From 1986 to 1989, Chinese military sales to Third World countries exceeded those of Britain, France and Germany combined.

China sold the deadly Silkworm missiles to both Iran

and Iraq. It has sold short-range M-11 missiles to Pakistan and signed contracts to sell medium-range M-9 missiles to Syria. It is currently selling what it calls civilian nuclear technology to Algeria and Iran.

China participated in the July 1991 Paris meeting on weapons proliferation, its first involvement in any discussion of its arms trade. China took another step to improve its international image in 1992 when it signed the Nuclear Nonproliferation Treaty of 1968.

ADMINISTRATION POLICY

■ **MFN.** President Bush continues to support the extension of MFN status to China without conditions: "There is no doubt in my mind that if we present China's leaders with an ultimatum on MFN, the result will be weakened ties to the West and further repression. The end result will not be progress on human rights, arms control, or trade. Anyone familiar with recent Chinese history can attest that the most brutal and protracted periods of repression took place precisely when China turned inward, against the world." The Bush Administration argues that revoking MFN would hurt the very forces in China that are working for reform.

In a letter to Congress in March 1992, the President outlined the Administration's future strategy toward China: the U.S. "comprehensive policy of engagement on several separate fronts invites China's leadership to act responsibly without leaving any doubts about the consequences of Chinese misdeeds."

POLICY CHOICES

1. MFN STATUS:
A. Maintain MFN privileges and leverage they provide over Chinese policy in areas of concern to U.S.

OR

B. Withhold MFN privileges until China abandons restrictive trade practices, suspends arms sales to the Middle East and observes human rights.

2. HUMAN RIGHTS:
A. Make human rights centerpiece of U.S. China policy.
                                    OR
B. Avoid stressing human-rights issue because this might damage relations with Beijing and result in loss of influence for the U.S.

SELECT BIBLIOGRAPHY

Bush, George, "China's MFN Status." *US Department of State Dispatch,* March 9, 1992, p. 189. Text of the President's letter vetoing legislation placing conditions on the renewal of China's MFN trade status.

"China." *Current History,* Sept. 1991. Entire issue devoted to Chinese policies and problems.

Harding, Harry, *A Fragile Relationship: The United States and China Since 1972.* Washington, D.C., The Brookings Institution, 1992. Survey of Sino-American relations since Nixon's opening to China.

Joseph, William A., ed., *China Briefing, 1991.* Boulder, Colo., Westview Press, 1992. Seven chapters written by experts examine the major issues in China after Tiananmen.

11

Global Warming

✔ *Do you favor or oppose legislation requiring the U.S. to stabilize carbon dioxide emissions at 1990 levels by the year 2000?*

✔ *Do you agree or disagree with the Administration's policy on global warming?*

✔ *Is it possible to reduce greenhouse gases without losing jobs?*

✔ *Would you be willing to pay higher taxes on electricity and gasoline?*

BASIC FACTS

■ Main greenhouse gases: carbon dioxide (50%), chlorofluorocarbons (20%), methane (16%), ozone (8%), nitrous oxide (6%).

■ Major greenhouse-gas producers (1989 figures): U.S.,17.8%; former U.S.S.R., 13.6%; China, 9.1%; Japan, 4.7%; India, 4.1%; Brazil, 3.9%; Germany, 3.4%; Britain, 2.2%; Mexico, 2.0%; Indonesia, 1.7%; Canada, 1.7%; Italy, 1.6%.

■ Human-activity-caused greenhouse gases: energy production (49%); industry (24%); deforestation (14%); agriculture (13%).

BACKGROUND

The average world temperature has risen about 1° F in the last 100 years. The planet has been warmer in the last decade than during any other since record-keeping began just over a century ago. Most scientists believe the rise in temperature is the result of gases produced by human activity, which are accumulating in the atmosphere and trapping heat, much like the glass in a greenhouse keeps heat inside. This so-called greenhouse effect occurs naturally and is what has made the earth warm enough to support life as we know it. However, many researchers believe that continued production of greenhouse gases at current levels may have devastating consequences. The Intergovernmental Panel on Climate Change (IPCC), the main international body gathering data on global warming, predicts that the planet's average temperature, now 60° F, may rise 3° F to 8° F over the next 100 years. If this occurred, temperature zones and rainfall patterns would change, flooding coastal regions and low-lying nations. Many species of plants and animals would be wiped out, and food supplies and energy production would be disrupted.

Not everyone is convinced that global warming is a threat. Some question the scientific data on which current projections of a warming trend are based. Nor does everyone agree that there is a link between global warming

Major Greenhouse-Gas Producers (1989)

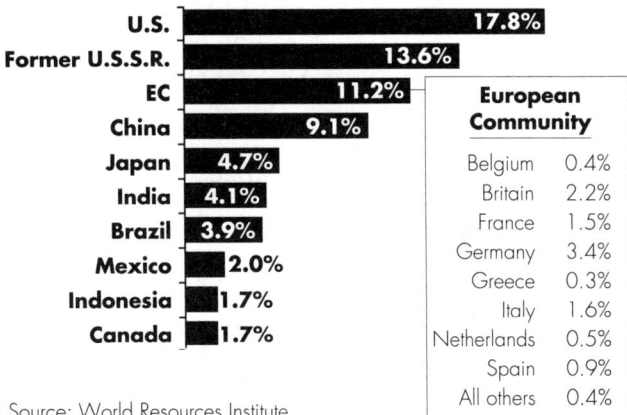

U.S.	17.8%
Former U.S.S.R.	13.6%
EC	11.2%
China	9.1%
Japan	4.7%
India	4.1%
Brazil	3.9%
Mexico	2.0%
Indonesia	1.7%
Canada	1.7%

European Community	
Belgium	0.4%
Britain	2.2%
France	1.5%
Germany	3.4%
Greece	0.3%
Italy	1.6%
Netherlands	0.5%
Spain	0.9%
All others	0.4%

Source: World Resources Institute

and industrialization. There are those who believe natural climate fluctuations, solar flares or volcanic activity may be responsible. Nevertheless, most of the international community considers global warming one of the most pressing transnational problems and agrees that, despite uncertainties about how much or how fast and with what consequences, global warming is a great enough risk to justify preventive steps.

Human activity (burning coal, oil and natural gas for heating, cooling, industry, transportation, etc., and deforestation) generates carbon dioxide (CO_2), which accounts for about half of all greenhouse gases. If current energy-use trends continue, CO_2 emissions worldwide could more than double in 40 years. Concentrations of CO_2 in the atmosphere are 25% higher today than they were 100 years ago.

■ **OZONE DEPLETION:** Chlorofluorocarbons (CFCs), which are used in refrigeration, air-conditioning, solvents and fire suppressants, in addition to contributing to global warming, are responsible for another major problem: the destruction of ozone in the atmosphere. While ozone at ground level produces smog and causes respiratory problems, in the stratosphere it helps block ultraviolet radiation from the sun that can produce skin cancer and eye disease, impair the immune system, reduce crops and lower fish and timber harvests.

Scientists began warning that CFCs were destroying the ozone in the early 1970s. In 1985 they first observed a large hole in the ozone shield over Antarctica that has recurred every winter since. That discovery led to the signing of the Montreal Protocol of 1987, which provided for a 50% reduction in the industrialized countries' production and use of five of the most harmful CFCs by the end of the century. In 1989, the timetable was speeded up, with 80 nations calling for an end to all production of CFCs by the year 2000.

In early 1992, American and European scientists announced the startling discovery of alarming concentrations of CFCs over the North Pole similar to those that

UN DEVELOPMENT PROGRAMME
CHOICES MAGAZINE/MICHAEL DALCERRO

are believed to be depleting the ozone shield over Antarctica. The possible depletion of the protective ozone layer over the Northern Hemisphere could expose densely populated areas of Britain, Scandinavia, Russia, North America and elsewhere to higher doses of utraviolet radiation. The new data prompted still another change of schedule: the European nations set the end of 1994 as their new deadline for phasing out CFCs and other ozone-destroying chemicals, such as halons, carbon tetrachloride and methyl chloroform, and the U.S. moved up its date to Dec. 31, 1995.

■ **WHAT TO DO ABOUT GLOBAL WARMING?** A reduction in greenhouse-gas emissions could be achieved by changing the types of fuel nations use to meet their energy needs and by using fuel more efficiently. Energy sources that produce few or no emissions of greenhouse gases include rivers (hydroelectric), the sun (solar), heat contained below the earth's surface (geothermal), wind, and decaying plant matter (biomass). The U.S. currently depends on these sources for less than 10% of its energy. Petroleum supplies 40.8% of U.S. needs, coal, 22.6%, natural gas, 22.3%, and nuclear energy, 6.8%.

The U.S. is also one of the least efficient users of energy. With less than 5% of the world's population, it consumes about one quarter of the world's energy and accounts for close to one fifth of greenhouse gases. Americans use twice as much energy per capita as Germans and Japanese. The European Community is considering a tax on all fossil fuels—coal, oil and gas—in order to cut energy consumption and encourage efficiency. There is not much support for an energy tax in the U.S., particularly in an election year. Opponents say it would cost jobs, raise prices and slow economic growth. Unofficial studies by U.S. Environmental Protection Agency analysts, on the other hand, indicate that if the revenue from an energy tax were offset by a tax credit for business investment, it would stimulate national economic growth.

■ **AN INTERNATIONAL CONVENTION:** Signing a legally binding international treaty to slow global warming and climate change was one of the main goals of the Earth Summit, formally the United Nations Conference on Environment and Development (Unced), held in Rio de Janeiro, Brazil, in June 1992. The conference, the largest international gathering in history, was attended by more than 100 heads of state. Recommendations by the IPCC, established in 1988 under the auspices of the UN World Meteorological Organization and the UN Environment Program, formed the basis of the treaty signed in Rio.

About two dozen developed nations, including the members of the European Community and Japan, wanted the convention to require the world community to stabilize CO_2 emissions at 1990 levels by the year 2000. The U.S. and a number of developing nations opposed specific targets and timetables. The Bush Administration said too little was known about the potential risks and consequences of global warming and about ways to offset it to justify mandatory targets and expensive remedial action. In the end a compromise was reached calling for voluntary compliance with a set of goals.

Estimates of the cost and effect of emissions-reducing measures vary greatly. The Bush Administration says cutting CO_2 emissions would cost tens of billions of dollars annually, eliminate millions of jobs and slow economic growth. A study by the Department of Energy, released in Dec. 1991, concluded that reducing carbon dioxide emissions by 20% from 1990 levels would cost $95 billion annually by 2000.

ASK THE CANDIDATES:
SHOULD THE U.S. GO TO THE EARTH SUMMIT?

Ohman/The Oregonian
Reprinted by permission Tribune Media Services.

Supporters of emissions-cutting measures, among them some government analysts, environmentalists, business leaders and economists, say they would lead to more efficient energy use, making U.S. industry in the long run more competitive internationally and creating savings that could be invested in other productive sectors. A study coordinated by the Union of Concerned Scientists concluded that cutting CO_2 emissions aggressively over the next 40 years could cost the economy about $2.7 trillion for investment in technology and infrastructure but it could save consumers and industry $5 trillion in fuel and electricity costs, with a net savings of $2.3 trillion. According to economist William R. Cline of the Institute for International Economics, a failure to act now on global warming could cost the U.S. economy a long-term loss of at least 6% in gross domestic product.

Another point at issue in Rio was the developing nations' demand that the industrialized countries provide them with funds and the technology to reduce greenhouse-gas emissions and implement other environmental measures to support sustainable development (development that does not adversely affect the environment and interfere with future growth). The wealthier nations currently provide the poorer nations development assistance totaling $55 billion annually. Maurice F. Strong, secretary-general of UNCED, has said that development that is sustainable would require an additional $70 billion a year. (The principal international body for distributing environmental aid is the Global Environmental Facility (GEF), a $1.5 billion fund set up by the World Bank, the UN Development Program and the UN Environment Program.)

The European Community members, Canada and Scandinavia have pledged to provide more aid to preserve the environment in the developing world although they have not specified the amount. Most of the developed nations, with the exception of the U.S., are also willing to make available their technology.

The Administration had refused to commit itself to providing more aid, but in a concession in Feb. 1992 it agreed to provide an additional $75 million: $50 million for the GEF and $25 million to help individual nations measure their greenhouse-gas emissions, inventory their forests and determine climate baselines to be able to gauge future changes.

The majority of delegates to the Rio conference attacked the U.S. stand on the global-warming treaty. Other critics included the Democratic presidential candidates. Arkansas Gov. Bill Clinton supported firm targets for stabilizing emissions. He said that as President he would raise automobile fuel-efficiency standards, redirect spending toward renewable resources and reduce energy consumption by at least one fourth. But Clinton acknowledged that his own environmental record as governor is flawed. Faced with short-term trade-offs between jobs and the environment in his depressed state, he chose jobs.

ADMINISTRATION POLICY

President George Bush, in his address to Unced in June, stated: "America's record on environmental protection is second to none, so I did not come here to apologize," and he called for a "prompt start" to carrying out the global warming and other accords. He challenged other nations to join the U.S. by Jan. 1, 1993, in detailing plans for controlling greenhouse-gas emissions. As part of what the Administration calls its no-regrets policy, it is implementing those measures that not only reduce emissions but also produce other benefits to society. Policies that stress conservation and greater energy efficiency, for example, are cost-effective whether or not the threat of global warming becomes real. The Administration has proposed raising energy-efficiency standards for appliances and equipment, giving electric utilities incentives to improve efficiency rather than build new coal-burning power plants, increasing federal purchases of alternative-fuel vehicles, capturing methane from landfills and planting more trees.

The Administration agrees that combined emissions of all greenhouse gases should be cut, and it maintains that it has taken a big step in this direction by phasing out CFCs, which, it says, will offset any increase in CO_2 emissions. A recent report by the UN Environment Program challenges the Administration's logic. CFCs can have both a direct climate-warming effect and an indirect cooling effect. The latter occurs because CFCs contribute to the destruction of the ozone shield, which appears to let some heat escape.

POLICY CHOICE

SET SPECIFIC TARGETS AND A TIMETABLE FOR CUTTING EMISSIONS OF GREENHOUSE GASES TO 1990 LEVELS BY THE YEAR 2000.

YES. Cutting emissions is beneficial regardless of whether the threats posed by global warming ever materialize. Using energy more efficiently to cut emissions will save billions of dollars, create jobs and make the U.S. more competitive internationally. The U.S. must set an example as the world's richest nation and the biggest producer of greenhouse gases. Not taking action will be far more costly in the long run in terms of lost economic productivity, the destruction of resources, environmental degradation and social dislocation.

NO. Not enough is known about the causes and effects of global warming to commit the world community to specific timetables and targets to reduce CO_2 emissions. Implementing such cuts will hamper economic growth, eliminate jobs and cost billions of dollars. What is needed instead of regulations are incentives to industry to develop sound technology. The U.S. is displaying world leadership by implementing voluntary measures to cut emissions. Fears of environmental disaster are exaggerated and unfounded.

SELECT BIBLIOGRAPHY

The Bulletin of the Atomic Scientists, June 1992, pp. 29–39. Two opposing views on global warming: "Global Warming: The Worst Case," by Jeremy Leggett, and "Warming Theories Need Warning Label," by S. Fred Singer.

"Climate Change: A Global Concern," *World Resources 1990–91: A Guide to the Global Environment.* New York, Oxford University Press, 1990, pp. 11–31. Special chapter on global warming and solutions, with comparative charts.

"Global Warming and the Environment: Forecast Disaster?" *Great Decisions 1990,* pp. 79–88. New York, Foreign Policy Association, 1990. Overview of global warming, energy use, international action and U.S. policy.

12

International Drug Trafficking

✔ *Is the U.S. winning or losing the war on drugs?*

✔ *Which should receive priority: stopping the supply of drugs or reducing Americans' demand?*

✔ *Is legalization of drugs the answer?*

BASIC FACTS

■ The U.S. is the largest drug market in the world; it absorbs 80% of the world cocaine supply.

■ In 1990, 26 million Americans spent more than $40 billion to buy and use illicit drugs.

■ Drugs may cost the U.S. as much as $176 billion a year in crime, law enforcement, prison maintenance, lost economic production, work place accidents, medical care, etc.

■ Revenues from the international drug trade are estimated to be between $100 billion and $500 billion a year, more than is generated by the petroleum industry.

BACKGROUND

The illicit drug trade threatens the stability of governments. In Colombia, drug traffickers have waged a virtual civil war against the government. More than 1,000 people have been murdered, including a justice minister, an attorney general, a presidential candidate and hundreds of judges, prosecutors and police. Traffickers in Colombia and elsewhere corrupt or intimidate those in authority, undermining public confidence in government. The drug trade allegedly also has helped support left-wing, anti-government insurgents—the Revolutionary Armed Forces in Colombia and the Shining Path in Peru—who reportedly charge a "war tax" to protect growers from the police and the army and negotiate higher prices from coca-leaf buyers.

The global environment is also severely affected by the drug trade. Land is being cleared for new plantations, contributing to deforestation and soil erosion. Rivers, rain forests and farmland are being contaminated by the pesticides used to grow coca, by the chemicals used to process it and by the herbicides used to eradicate it.

■ **SOURCES:** Much of the world's **heroin** comes from opium poppies grown in the Golden Triangle, a mountainous area joining Myanmar (formerly Burma), Thailand and Laos, and from the Golden Crescent in Southwest Asia, which includes parts of Pakistan, Afghanistan, Iran and Lebanon. Mexico produces one third to one half of the heroin consumed in the U.S.; poppy growing also is on the rise in Guatemala and Colombia.

Cocaine comes from South America. Peru and Bolivia grow most of the coca leaves (together they account for more than 80% of the world's total coca acreage). Colombia has been the main processor and exporter of cocaine since the 1970s; in the 1980s it became the third leading grower of coca as well. Most of the **marijuana** consumed in the U.S. is grown in Mexico and Colombia and, to a lesser extent, in Jamaica and Belize.

■ **ECONOMICS:** Profits from the international drug trade are astronomical. Just one cache of cocaine—22 tons seized in a Los Angeles suburb in 1989—had an estimated street value of $6 billion to $7 billion, a sum exceeding the gross national products of more than 100 countries.

"Oh? Well, then . . . take me to your front-runner!"

The drug industry also is a major employer: U.S. diplomats have estimated that up to 30% of Bolivia's work force and 15% of Peru's derive their income directly or indirectly from narcotics. While most of the profits go to the drug lords, peasants can earn much more from coca and poppies than from traditional crops. In 1985, for example, coca growers could earn $9,000 from 2.2 acres of land, while citrus growers earned only $500 from a comparable plot. Pakistani farmers earn 10 times more from poppies than from tobacco and fruit. "Narcodollars" contribute substantially to Bolivia's and Peru's export earnings, but they also distort local economies, add to inflation, and retard economic development by channeling resources away from nation-building enterprises.

More than 26 million Americans spent over $40 billion to buy illicit drugs in 1990. The use of drugs ranging from marijuana to LSD became widespread in the 1960s, especially among the youth of all social classes. New criminal organizations emerged, and drug trafficking became an international issue. The drug wave began to subside in the 1970s, with the exception of cocaine. Seeking to boost sales, in the mid-1980s drug dealers introduced crack, a low-cost, smokable and highly addictive cocaine derivative that produces an instant euphoria. Sales took off, especially among the poorer sectors of society, which also became the main victims of rising crack-related crime, violence, drug gangs and health problems. Cocaine use peaked in 1985: the number of illegal users has fallen from 23 million that year to about 13 million today.

The U.S. appears to be an exception to the general trend. The number of drug users is on the rise in Western Europe and many developing regions, including Africa (which is increasingly used as a transit route to Europe) and drug-producing nations in Latin America and Asia. The number of drug addicts in the former Soviet Union has almost doubled since the mid-1980s and is rising in Eastern Europe and China.

■ **HISTORY:** Narcotics have been used for thousands of years for purposes ranging from medicinal to spiritual. Peruvian and Bolivian Indians, for example, traditionally chew coca leaves or brew them for tea to reduce sensations of hunger and cold. The first international convention to regulate drugs, drawn up to address the opium problem, was signed in 1912. After World War I, the League of Nations assumed a major regulatory function, a mandate passed on to the United Nations after World War II. The most recent international instrument is the UN Convention Against Illicit Traffic in Narcotic Drugs and Psychotropic Substances, approved in Vienna in 1988 and put into force in Nov. 1990. The convention defines narcotic and money-laundering offenses, requires governments to monitor drug money and chemicals used in drug processing, and obliges states to prosecute or extradite individuals accused of trafficking.

The main international drug agency is the Vienna-based UN International Drug Control Program (Undcp), created in 1991 by consolidating three existing UN drug agencies. The bulk of funding for UN efforts comes from voluntary contributions.

U.S. DRUG POLICIES

The U.S. spends more money to fight drugs than any other nation in the world. Expenditures have risen steadily, from $82 million in 1969 to $2.7 billion in 1986 to $12.7 billion requested for fiscal year 1993. A dozen principal executive departments help combat the drug problem, including the Department of Justice, the Drug Enforcement Administration (DEA), the Coast Guard (part of the Department of Transportation), the Customs Service (part of the Treasury Department) and the Defense Department. All international drug-fighting activities are coordinated through the Department of State's Bureau of International Narcotics Matters.

Over 70% of federal antidrug money goes to the criminal justice system, including law enforcement, the courts and prisons. The next biggest allocations go for interdiction, followed by drug-treatment programs and by education.

A major issue in the U.S. drug debate is whether to focus on eliminating the supply of drugs by eradicating crops, knocking out processing labs, interdicting shipments and arresting traffickers, or whether to concentrate on reducing demand at home through education, drug treatment and rehabilitation, and local law enforcement. Although the U.S. has traditionally relied on supply-side strategies, in recent years the demand side has received increased attention, if not much more funding. In 1990, 71% of antidrug money went to tackle supplies and only 29% went to programs aimed at reducing demand.

ADMINISTRATION POLICY

In Sept. 1989, President George Bush unveiled his first National Drug Control Strategy, which aimed to cut dangerous drugs entering the U.S. by 50% over a 10-year period. A key aspect is the "Andean initiative," a $2.3 billion, five-year program of U.S. economic and military aid that stresses disrupting cocaine production and criminal-trafficking organizations in Bolivia, Colombia and Peru. The program evolved from a drug summit meeting in Cartagena, Colombia, in Feb. 1990. At a second summit in San Antonio, Tex., in Feb. 1992, Ecuador, Mexico and Venezuela joined the antidrug effort. The U.S. has encouraged Andean nations to increase their military participation in antidrug activities. It also shifted the focus from eradication and low-level interdictions to dismantling the drug-trafficking organizations.

In 1991, the U.S. for the first time provided economic assistance to develop alternatives to coca production. The aid is conditioned on countries' making certain efforts to curtail trafficking. (For years Congress has required the President to certify that nations are cooperating with U.S. antidrug efforts and to cut off aid to those that are not. However, the President could certify a nation even if it was not cooperating on the grounds of overriding security interests. This occurred in Central America and Afghanistan, where anti-Communist factions receiving U.S. aid were reportedly involved in drug trafficking.)

The Administration says that in 1990, for the first time in a decade, acreage of coca under cultivation did not increase and attributes the fact to the success of the offensive against drug-trafficking organizations. It also states that seizures, arrests and confiscations of assets have increased. However, the results of President Bush's drug policies are still unclear. Bob Martinez, head of the federal Office of National Drug Control Policy, compares efforts to cut drug production and trafficking to "squeezing a balloon." The crackdown in Colombia has led to new processing labs springing up in Bolivia, Brazil and Peru. Increased surveillance of Mexican and Caribbean drug routes has shifted transshipment to Central America, Venezuela and even Argentina. Panama, for years an important drug center, appears to be experiencing an increase in trafficking despite the 1989 U.S. invasion and the arrest and trial in Miami of former Panamanian strongman Gen. Manuel Antonio Noriega on charges of drug trafficking, money laundering and racketeering.

POLICY CHOICES

1. FOCUS RESOURCES ON ELIMINATING ILLEGAL DRUG SUPPLY.

YES. As long as addictive drugs such as cocaine and opium are available, there will be a demand for them. Therefore, priority must be given to cutting off supplies. International economic and military cooperation through efforts such as the Andean initiative can achieve that goal.

NO. The supply-curtailing policy has been ineffective and has created much resentment among drug-producing nations. Despite eradication efforts, cocaine production increased tenfold between 1979 and 1989. Crop substitution that sometimes accompanies eradication is not always effective or even possible, especially in places such as Afghanistan and Laos, with poor roads, few markets and no other crop as easy to transport and as resistant to deterioration as opium.

2. LEGALIZE THE SALE AND USE OF DRUGS.

[Prohibition appears to reduce consumption but increase criminal activity, while legalization is likely to increase consumption, at least in the short-term, but decrease criminal activity. The prohibition of alcohol in the U.S. in the 1920s and 1930s was abandoned after a decade when the country decided the health benefits of reduced consumption did not justify the increase in crime. However, some question whether the same argument can be applied to a much more addictive drug such as cocaine.]

YES. Previous drug-fighting programs have failed. Therefore, it is time to try a radical new solution. Legalization would reduce law enforcement costs and provide a new source of tax revenue, which could be used for education and rehabilitation. (Supporters include former Secretary of State George P. Shultz and economist Milton Friedman.)

NO. Certain drugs are so addictive that making them readily available through legalization would create a drug-use epidemic. The expenditures saved on law enforcement would simply be shifted to health care. (Opponents include President Bush and most of Congress.)

3. INCREASE SPENDING ON DRUG EDUCATION AND TREATMENT PROGRAMS.

YES. The U.S. should reorder its priorities and place at least as much emphasis on drug education and treatment as on law enforcement.

NO. Education and treatment programs may produce results in the long run, but they do not address the immediate problem, which is to eliminate the drug trade.

SELECT BIBLIOGRAPHY

Bush, George, "Two Years After Cartagena: Assessing Accomplishments and Plans." *US Department of State Dispatch,* March 2, 1992, pp. 145–53. Excerpts from the President's opening statement at the San Antonio drug summit, Feb. 27, 1992. (Most of the issue is devoted to aspects of the international drug trade.)

Collett, Merrill, "The Cocaine Connection: Drug Trafficking and Inter-American Relations." *Headline Series* No. 290. New York, Foreign Policy Association, Fall 1989.

The Global Connection: New International Approaches for Controlling Narcotic Drugs. A Report of the Global Policy Project, United Nations Association of the United States of America, 485 Fifth Ave., New York, NY 10017, 1991. Also recommended is the UNA-USA's briefing book, *Breaking the Drug Chain: Options for International Policy on Narcotic Drugs* by Jeffrey Laurenti. New York, 1990.

Index

A

Afghanistan, 76, 112, 116
Africa, Horn of, 80
Agricultural Trade Development and Assistance Act (1954), 58
agriculture, 25–26, 28, 102, 112
    food distribution, 46, 48
    free trade, 25
    restrictions, 27
    subsidies, 25–26, 30
AID. See U.S. Agency for International Development
Algeria, 72, 100
"America First," 6–7
Andean initiative, 55, 62, 115–6
Anderson, Lisa, 72
Angola, 76, 79, 80
Arab-Israeli peace talks, 68–69, 72–7
Argentina, 21, 25, 29
Armenia, 45, 47
arms
    Black Sea fleet, 47
    control, 70, 100
    conventional forces, 14, 15, 16–17
    cutbacks, 14–23
    embargo, 67
    M-9 missile, 100
    M-11 missile, 100
    military budget, Japan, 34
    nonconventional, 8
    proliferation, 8, 71–6, 99–100
    Seawolf attack submarine, 16, 18
    Silkworm missile, 99
    Stealth bomber, 16
    Strategic Defense Initiative, 16
    unilateral reductions, 20
    See also nuclear weapons.
Arms Control Association, 71
Asean Free Trade Area, 29–30
Aspin, Les, 16, 18, 19, 51
al-Assad, Hafez, 68
Australia, 25, 36
Austria, 27–28
automobile industry, 10, 27, 28, 36–37, 108
Azerbaijan, 45, 47

B

Bahrain, 71
Baker, James A., 3d, 69, 70, 72, 73, 81, 83
Bangladesh, 80
Bartley, Robert L., 50
Belarus, 21, 43, 45, 51
Belize, 112
Bolivia, 112, 114, 115, 116
Bovard, James P., 27
Brazil, 21, 79, 82, 102, 116
Britain, 21–22, 35, 48, 76, 99, 102
Brookings Institution, 16
Brown, Jerry, 16, 18, 26
Brunei, 29
Buchanan, Patrick J., 7, 9, 18, 26
budget deficit. See economy
Burkhalter, Holly, 98
Burma. See Myanmar
Bush, George, 11, 16, 20, 29, 30, 36, 48, 49, 51, 52, 59, 65, 68, 71, 72, 76, 81, 95, 108, 115, 116

Administration, 8, 16, 30, 52, 58, 62, 68, 70, 72, 73, 79, 81, 83, 91–2, 95, 100, 106, 108, 109, 115–6

C

Cambodia, 79, 80, 81, 86–92
  free elections, 89
  invaded, 87–9
  peace talks, 89
  refugees, 80, 89, 91
Camp David accords, 61
Canada, 24, 28, 34, 48, 102, 108
CARE, 58
Carter, Jimmy, 95
Center for Defense Information, 20–21
Cheney, Dick, 18
China, People's Republic of, 21, 34, 39, 45, 60, 76, 79, 89, 90, 94–101, 102, 114
  and Cambodia, 89
  and Tibet, 97
  and Vietnam, 90
  arms control, 99, 100
  human rights, 60, 95, 99
  military budget, 99
  MFN status, 95–96, 100
  normalization of relations, 95
  nuclear technology sales, 100
  prison-made exports, 99
  sanctions, 95
  seat in UN, 94
  Tiananmen Square, 95, 97
  trade, 100
CIS. See Commonwealth of Independent States
Cline, William R., 107
Clinton, Bill, 8, 16, 18, 27, 37, 49, 61, 108
collective security. See global interests
Colombia, 111, 112, 115, 116

summit meeting, 115
Commonwealth of Independent States, 20, 21, 40, 43, 45, 46, 58–59, 62, 114
  Black Sea fleet, 47
  coup attempt, 46, 48
  currency stabilization program, 49
  defense, 47
  economic reform, 47, 50
  enforcement of contracts, 50
  free-market reforms, 48
  property rights, 50
  territorial disputes, 47
  Treaty of Union, 46
conflicts, regional, 8
  resolution of, 11, 15–16, 81
Congress
  antidrug efforts, 116
  assertive role in foreign policy, 87
  base closings, 18
  budget deficits, 8–9
  foreign aid, 58–59
  trade restrictions, 26
consumer electronics, 10
Council on Competitiveness, 38

D

Dalai Lama, 97
defense, 8
  budget, 14–23
  conversion, 20, 48
Defense Department, 58, 115
democracy, 8, 11, 41, 52, 62, 76
  cut short, 72, 95
  election-monitoring, 79, 80
Deng Xiaoping, 95, 99
Denmark, 27
Department of Agriculture, 58
Department of Energy, 106

Department of Justice, 115

Department of State, 58, 115

Department of Transportation, 115

developing countries, 11, 41, 56, 57, 61, 62, 72, 76, 79, 82, 99–100, 107, 114

Djerejian, Edward P., 73

domestic needs, 5–13

    See also defense

drugs, 111–6

    abuse, 5

    antidrug funding, 114, 115

    Bureau of International Narcotics Matters, 115

    Coast Guard, 115

    Customs Service, 115

    Drug Enforcement Administration (DEA), 115

    economics of, 113–4

    National Drug Control Strategy, 115

    Office of National Drug Control Policy, 116

    social costs, 111, 113

    sources, 112

    trafficking, 10, 111–6

    UN Convention Against Illicit Traffic in Narcotic Drugs and Psychotropic Substances, 114

    UN International Drug Control Program (Undcp), 114

    war on, 62, 114–8

Dunkel, Arthur, 26

E

Eastern Europe, 55, 61, 62, 96, 114

Economic Support Fund, 58

economy, 9–10, 24, 106, 112

    balanced-budget amendment, 9

    budget deficit, 8

    defense budget, 14–23

    gross national product (GNP), 33, 94

    Omnibus Budget Reconciliation Act, 9, 19

    See also global economy

Ecuador, 115

Egypt, 55, 61, 62, 68, 69, 71, 72, 76, 82

El Salvador, 79, 80

employment, 18–19, 24, 27, 30, 36, 49, 106, 108, 113

energy, 102, 104, 106–7, 108, 109

Enterprise for the Americas Initiative, 28–29

environment, 46, 62, 112

    environmental safeguards, 28, 107

    Global Environmental Facility (GEF), 108

    natural resources, 10, 62, 70, 102, 108, 109

environmentalists, 28, 107

    Environmental Defense Fund, 28

    Sierra Club, 28

Estonia, 43

Ethiopia, 59

Europe, 15, 17–18, 50, 56, 114

European Community (EC), 24, 25–26, 27–28, 81, 105, 106, 108

European Economic Area (EEA), 27–28

European Free Trade Association (EFTA), 27

European Parliament, 28

exports, 56, 61

    Bolivian drugs, 112

    China, 94

    Japan, 33, 37

    jobs, 24

    Latin American, 29

    Peruvian drugs, 112

F

family planning, 56, 59–60
Fang Lizhu, 95, 98
Finland, 27–28
foreign aid, 34, 49–50, 52, 55–64, 81
  agricultural, 48
  as % of GNP in U.S.
  bilateral, 58, 62
  development assistance, 57, 108
  economic, 45, 57, 61, 62, 115
  food (Food for Peace), 57–58, 61
  humanitarian, 19, 50, 56, 57–58, 62, 73
  limits on, 19
  Marshall Plan, 43, 50, 55–56
  military, 57, 68
  multilateral, 68
  reconstruction in Vietnam, 86
  reform, 60–61
  security assistance, 56–57
  technical assistance, 48, 50, 56, 59, 108
Foreign Assistance Act (1961), 60
  "New Directions" initiative, 61
Foreign Policy Association, 49, 73
France, 21, 40, 48, 76, 82, 99
free market, 43, 48, 52, 62
free trade, 8, 11, 26–27, 29, 30, 36, 37, 61
Front for Islamic Salvation (FIS), 72

G

Gaza Strip, 59, 69
Gelatt, Timothy A., 98
General Agreement on Tariffs and Trade (GATT), 25–26, 30
  Uruguay Round, 25–26, 30

Geneva Conference (1954), 86–7
Georgia, 45, 47
Gephardt, Richard A., 25, 36, 96
Germany, 10, 24, 48, 81, 82, 99, 102
  East, 38, 48, 81
  West, 38, 81
Ghali, Boutros, 76
glasnost, 46
Glaspie, April, 68
global concerns, 5–13
  collective security, 15–16, 27, 71, 73, 76, 83
  international consensus, 8, 11
  multilateral actions, 8, 41, 65, 70
  pollution, 10, 28
  terrorism, 10
  unilateral actions, 7
global economy, 10, 36, 41
  U.S. share of, 10
Global Environmental Facility (GEF), 108
global warming, 10, 102–10
  effects of, 102–5
  energy, 102, 104, 106–7, 108, 109
  greenhouse effect, 103
  greenhouse gases, 102, 105, 107, 109
  industrialization, 104
  Intergovernmental Panel on Climate Change (IPCC), 103, 106
  UN Environment Program (UNEP), 106, 108, 109
  Union of Concerned Scientists, 107
  See also environment
Golan Heights, 69
Golden Crescent, 112
Golden Triangle, 112
Gorbachev, Mikhail S., 20, 46–47, 48, 76
Greece, 55

Group of Seven (G-7), 45, 48, 49, 52, 59

Guatemala, 112

Gulf Cooperation Council (GCC), 71, 73

Gulf war. See Persian Gulf war.

H

Haiti, 80

Henry L. Stimson Center, 81

Heritage Foundation, 7

Hills, Carla, 99

Ho Chi Minh, 86

Hong Kong, 90, 96

hostages, 73

House Armed Services Committee, 16

House Foreign Affairs Committee, 60

Hrawi, Elias, 68

human rights, 52, 60, 79, 90, 95, 97–98

Human Rights Watch, 98

humanitarian aid, 19, 48, 50, 56, 57–58, 62, 73, 80

Hun Sen, 89, 91

Hussein, Saddam, 39, 65, 67, 68, 70, 73

I

ICBM. See intercontinental ballistic missile

Iceland, 27

India, 21, 45, 82, 102

Indochina, 86
    refugees, 86

Indonesia, 29, 102

industry, 18, 27, 28, 30, 36, 46, 102

Institute for International Economics, 107

intellectual property rights, 25, 98–99

Inter-American Development Bank, 58

intercontinental ballistic missile, 20

Intergovernmental Panel on Climate Change (IPCC), 103, 106

International Atomic Energy Agency, 21

International Court of Justice, 8, 76

international involvement, 6

International Monetary Fund (IMF), 11, 45, 49–50, 89

investment, 25, 27, 28, 34–35, 36, 38, 50, 52, 61

Iran, 67, 99, 112

Iran-Iraq War, 76

Iraq, 21–22, 65–68, 71, 73, 80, 100
    arms embargo, 67
    destruction of arms, 67
    sanctions, 65

Islamic revival, 71

isolationism, 6

Israel, 21, 55, 58–59, 61, 65, 68–70, 71, 72–7
    Gaza Strip, 59, 69
    Golan Heights, 69
    land for peace, 69, 72
    nuclear weapons, 71
    settlements, 70
    West Bank, 59, 69

Italy, 48, 102

J

Jackson-Vanik amendment, 95

Jamaica, 112

Japan, 10, 17, 24, 26, 33–42, 48, 61, 81, 82, 98, 102, 106
    foreign aid, 40, 48
    gross national product (GNP), 33
    military budget, 34

jobs. See employment
Johnson, Lyndon B., 15
Jordan, 69, 72

K

Kaifu, Toshiki, 39
Karnow, Stanley, 87
Kassebaum amendment, 76, 79
Kazakhstan, 21, 52
Kennedy, John F., 16
Khmer Rouge, 87–9, 91–2
    sanctuaries, 87
Khomeini, Ayatollah Ruhollah,
    72
Kimmitt, Robert, 96
Kohl, Helmut, 48, 49
Korean War, 34, 94
Kurdistan, 67
Kurds, 67, 71
Kurile Islands, 40
Kuwait, 39, 65, 67–68, 70, 71,
    73
Kyrgyzstan, 45

L

labor, 27, 28, 36, 113
Laos, 86, 92, 112
Latvia, 43
Lebanon, 79
Liechtenstein, 27
Lithuania, 43

M

Maastricht Treaty, 27
Malaysia, 29
Martinez, Bob, 116
Marshall Plan, 43, 50, 55–56
McNamara, Robert S., 15
Mexico, 10, 24, 28, 102, 112,
    115

MIAs (missing in action), 86, 91
Middle East, 16, 65–74
    peace conference, 68, 72
    See also individual countries.
Miyazawa, Kiichi, 36
Moldova, 45
most-favored-nation (MFN), 95–
    96
Multifiber Arrangement (MFA),
    27, 30
    See also trade.
Myanmar, 112

N

Namibia, 79, 80
National Academy of Sciences,
    20
National Drug Control Strategy,
    115
Nazarbayev, Nursultan, 51, 52
Netherlands, the, 27
new world order, 11, 29, 83
Nicaragua, 62, 79, 80
Nigeria, 82
Nixon, Richard M., 49, 52, 94
Noriega, Manuel Antonio, 116
North American Free Trade
    Agreement (Nafta), 28
North Atlantic Treaty Organiza-
    tion (NATO), 17–18, 55
"Northern Islands." See Kurile
    Islands
North Korea, 21–22, 82
Norway, 27
Nuclear Nonproliferation Treaty
    (NPT), 21–22, 51, 100
nuclear technology, spread of,
    21, 22, 43, 100
nuclear weapons, 20–21, 43, 45,
    50–51, 52, 71
    dismantling, 19, 51
    first use, 21
Nunn, Sam, 19, 51

O

Oman, 71
Omnibus Budget Reconciliation Act, 9, 19
Omnibus Trade and Competitiveness Act, 40
Operation Desert Storm, 70

P

Pakistan, 21, 100, 112, 113
Palestine, 80
Panama, 62, 116
Partnership for Business and Development, 62
Paris peace talks, 89
peace dividend, 8, 15, 19–20
peacekeeping, 68, 76–84
perestroika, 46
Pérez de Cuéllar, Javier, 83
Perot, H. Ross, 37
Persian Gulf war, 22, 39, 65, 67, 79, 82, 96
Peru, 112, 113, 114, 115, 116
Philippines, 29, 39, 55
Poland, 62
political violence, 15–16
pollution, 10, 28, 46
Pol Pot, 87
Portugal, 55
POWs (prisoners of war), 86, 87, 91
protectionism, 25, 26–27, 36–37

Q

Qatar, 71
Quayle, Dan, 40

R

Rabin, Yitzhak, 70
Reagan, Ronald, 60, 77

recession, 36, 49, 81
refugees, 67, 70, 80, 86, 89
Revolutionary Armed Forces, 112
Romania, 45
Russia, 21, 43, 45, 46, 47, 50, 76, 79, 82

S

Saudi Arabia, 68, 70, 71
Scandinavia, 108
Scowcroft, Brent, 95
security assistance, 56–57
Self-Defense Force, 34
Shamir, Yitzhak, 70
Shiite, 67
Shining Path, 112
Sihanouk, Prince Norodom, 89, 90, 91
Simon, Paul, 81
Singapore, 29
social needs, 19, 46, 48, 49, 50, 62, 67, 77, 113, 115
Somalia, 80
Son Sann, 89
South Africa, 21, 79
South Korea, 18, 39, 82
Soviet Union, 5, 6, 15, 18, 19, 43–54, 59, 77, 82
    See also Commonwealth of Independent States and individual states.
Star Wars. See Strategic Defense Initiative
State Department, 58
strategic arms reduction treaty (Start), 20, 51, 52
Strategic Defense Initiative, 16
Strong, Maurice F., 108
Super 301. See Omnibus Trade and Competitiveness Act
Sweden, 27–28
Switzerland, 27–28
Syria, 100

T

Taiwan, 94

Tajikistan, 45

Thailand, 29, 89, 112

Third World. See developing
countries.

Tiananmen Square, 95, 97, 98

Tibet, 97

trade, 10, 24–33, 34–35, 50, 61,
62, 96, 97, 100
  balance, 24, 25, 33, 36, 94,
    98
  barriers, 25, 26, 27, 28, 29,
    38, 40, 52, 61, 98, 99
  bilateral agreements, 26
  dumping, 35
  Jackson-Vanik amendment,
    95
  most-favored-nation (MFN),
    95–96
  Multifiber Arrangement, 27
  Omnibus Trade and
    Competitiveness Act, 40
  regional blocs, 27–30
  tariff rates, 25
  unfair practices, 26, 40

Treasury Department, 115

Tsongas, Paul E., 8

Turkey, 55, 67, 72

Turkmenistan, 45

U

Ukraine, 21, 43, 45, 46, 47, 51

Union of Concerned Scientists,
107

United Arab Emirates, 71

United Nations, 8, 11, 22, 65–68,
76–84, 90, 91
  budget, 77, 79
  Economic and Social Council
    (Ecosoc), 76
  election monitoring, 79
  fiscal reform, 77, 83

Food and Agriculture
  Organization (FAO), 76

funding for peacekeeping, 81

General Assembly, 11, 70,
  76, 83

International Labor Organization (ILO), 76

military forces, 82

Military Staff Committee, 82

Nobel Peace Prize, 80

Resolution 687, 67, 71

Resolution 688, 67

Secretariat, 76

Security Council, 16, 65, 67,
  79, 80, 81, 82, 83, 89, 96

UN Children's Fund
  (Unicef), 76, 79

UN Convention Against
  Illicit Traffic in Narcotic
  Drugs and Psychotropic
  Substances, 114

UN Development Program
  (UNDP), 58, 76, 79, 108

UN Environment Program
  (UNEP), 76, 106, 108,
  109

UN International Drug
  Control Program (Undcp),
  114

UN Population Fund
  (Unfpa), 59–60

UN Transitional Authority in
  Cambodia (Untac), 80, 90

World Health Organization
  (WHO), 76

U.S. Agency for International
  Development (AID), 58, 60,
  61, 62

Uruguay Round, 25

Uzbekistan, 45

V

Vance, Cyrus R., 81

Venezuela, 115, 116

Vietnam, 6, 86–92
  division of, 86

economic liberalization
program, 89

normalization of relations,
90, 91–2

POW/MIAs, 86, 87, 91

refugees, 90

syndrome, 87

trade embargo, 89, 92

war, 87

W

weaponry. See arms

West Bank, 59, 69

Western Sahara, 80

World Bank, 8, 11, 49, 58, 61,
76, 89, 92, 108

World Court. See International
Court of Justice.

Y

Yeltsin, Boris N., 20, 46, 48, 50,
79

Yugoslavia, 80, 81

Z

Zoellick, Robert B., 30

■ ■ ■ ■ ■ ■ ■ ■ ■ ■ ■ ■

A Valuable Resource for Both Teachers and Students and a way to keep up-to-date on key foreign policy topics in the news . . . .

Subscribe to the **HEADLINE SERIES,** published four times a year.

Each issue ● is about a major world area or topic
● is written by an expert
● is brief (usually 64 pages)
● is highly readable
● includes basic background, illustrations, discussion questions and an annotated reading list

---

Titles of Past Issues on Topics of Current Interest

297 *The Soviet Breakup and U.S. Foreign Policy,* by Allen Lynch

296 *Political Tides in the Arab World,* by Muhammad Muslih and Augustus Richard Norton

295 *U.S.S.R. and Eastern Europe: The Shattered Heartland,* by John C. Kimball (double issue: $7.50)

294 *The Two Koreas: On the Road to Reunification?* by Bruce Cumings

293 *U.S. Foreign Aid Policy—A Critique,* by Nicholas Eberstadt

292 *UN Peacekeepers: Soldiers with a Difference,* by Augustus Richard Norton and Thomas George Weiss

---

HOW TO ORDER
Price per copy: $4.00

Quantity Discounts

10–99	.25% off	500–999	.35% off
100–499	.30% off	1,000 or more	.40% off

Prepayment must accompany all orders.
Postage and handling: $2.50 first copy; $.50 each additional copy.

Subscriptions

One year—$15.00 ● Two years—$25.00 ● Three years—$30.00

Write or call for a **free** catalog.
Foreign Policy Association, c/o CUP Services
P.O. Box 6525, Ithaca, NY 14851
(800) 477-5836; Fax (607) 277-6292